INTRODUCTION:

THE NIGHTMARE

The American Dream has come true.

God help us all.

American civilization as we know it has been based on an ardent desire to overcome tradition through industry. It has conceived what it considers to be a "faith" in practicality, but far from being practical, the American faith is expedience. It has built a boat of special interests of both the right and the left and it does not desire that the boat be rocked. Both right and left are totally infected by the quest for profit, the idiocy of hypocrisy, and the temerity to try and pass off juvenile impulses as some great, grown-up agenda to be duplicated throughout the nation. Today's Liberal whines about corporate America while blogging on his corporately produced laptop, sipping a latte made with corporately-produced chemicals, wearing

clothing produced by a corporation, distributed by a corporation, or both;

and sits in a café owned by a large company, which is as corporate as

corporate can be. He likes to pretend that he is greater than the State that

coddles him. Indeed, the Liberal State needs him to foster that delusion.

For the Liberal, unable to stomach anything stronger than talking about

independence, is locked in codependency with that arch-enabler, the

Liberal State. The Liberal State, financed through the patronage of large

companies through their lobbyist operatives, plugs one unnecessary life-

support system after another into the Liberal who is convinced of his own

liberation.

The Conservative and the Republican have their own codependency with

the Liberal State. The Republican whines about traditional American

values while making room for illegal aliens to waltz over the border. Why?

Because he craves votes more than decency. In the industrialized,

assembly-line driven, instant packaged American Dream, quantity is more important than quality. Democracy as the two heads of the American Political Monster has conceived it is a sham. The Conservative will speak of traditional values, but he will allow corporations to walk all over the American Worker while social workers are allowed to do irreparable harm to the American Family. American greatness is a soulless, materialistic, socialistic technocracy with a touch of aristocratic, bureaucratic abortive nonsense.

Democracy is a sham fed to the gullible. It is nothing more than stale bread and second-rate circuses; a stylized ritual where people get to decide whether they want the criminals raping America to wear red lapel pins or blue ones. Does anyone really believe that their vote is going to change the quality of their life in any way? How can anyone persist in thinking that the smiling, one-eyed jack they're so desperately trying to put in office will represent the interests of the People? The public still trusts Democrats and Republicans, Liberals and Conservatives after nearly 300 years of organized lying, nepotism, scandal, and bureaucracy disguised as liberty.

It is time the American people woke up, grew up and stopped insisting that their government should be breast-feeding them. The milk is sour, maybe even poisoned. Americans are addicted to a toxin that isn't even going to get them high as it kills them. American "Democracy" is the greatest shell game on earth. It will be stopped, and that can happen in one of a few ways. Either the People will stand in support of a movement of Nationalist, Popular interests (unlikely, since Americans seldom want what's best for them as evinced by the very existence of the Obama Administration), or the system will degenerate into a bureaucratized gang-rape where the people are systematically exploited by first this party then that one (as is already the case) or the entire matrix of American civilization will collapse and come to resemble the jungle of Compton. America, it's time you grew up and faced the truth. The dream came true. Are you happy?

1.

THE COMING STORM AND THE COMING STATE

There is no doubt that we live in an age of darkness and the downfall of civilization. Mankind has perpetually misunderstood the nature of his own physics as an entity. Our materialism has pushed us into the belief that, since any physical object unsupported must fall then the human race, deprived of those structures and values that once upheld it, must inevitably fall into anarchy, perfidy, and cataclysmic destruction. This is rather like saying that an alcoholic *must* die of alcohol poisoning and that his decay into a wet-brain is unavoidable. It is the belief in an absolute historical inevitability, so ferociously clung to by the Marxists and all their subsidiary cults, that best characterizes the problem. They have always believed that since workers have been exploited and oppressed in virtually every society featuring any kind of industry beyond the level of stone tools, this must inevitably result in worldwide revolution and the total transformation of every single aspect of civilization to its opposite, whatever those aspects may have been. This is not the entirety of the symptoms of the age. It is an age without hope. Five minutes reading the commentary section of any social media or media website and you will see the rabid, irrational viciousness with which those who choose faith and belief are blasted by atheists and agnostics who are so horridly weak in their positions that they have come around to the perennial delusion that one's position can only be strengthened by attacking dissent. Our fundamental problems remain unsolved in spite of or perhaps because of public discourse. So far, every solution advocated has put forth violence, division, and hostility as fundamental components of its ideology. We know that this is an age without hope because its denizens only believe in the hostility of their solution to other viewpoints. All else is lip-service to fairy tale tolerance which is tossed aside in the face of an opposing view.

"Democracy"; a farce from its birth among the landholding classes of the ancient Mediterranean, has finally begun to drop its pretentions of representation. It is still a farce and a falsehood. If the People were being honest with themselves they would admit that they cling to it not out of enthusiasm for the idea but out of hope for a far-off day of equality, opportunity and representation that never seems to quite materialize without major hiccups that rock the entire system. The fact that nearly 250 years of blind faith in a system that merely exchanged aristocracy for bureaucracy has done nothing to deter that faith, which exemplifies the ancient doctrine that faith is irrational. However, the People still cling to the myth of Representation, even though they know in their hearts that they are not represented. How indeed can these professional liars and profiteers be said to represent the People? Income disparity alone should make the absurdity apparent. The average annual income for United States Senators and Congressmen is $174,000 per year, to say nothing of "other fees" our representatives collect from often nefarious, nebulous sources over the course of their more than checkered careers. The average working class salary of a United States citizen is $18,267.

How much bounty can there possibly be, then, for people who are allowed to enter this country illegally? Furthermore, we must not delude ourselves that our so-called representatives import the immigrant for any reason other than more votes, legal and otherwise. Who subsidizes these people? You do. A portion of all welfare monies given to these people goes back to their native countries, to poor relatives or terror groups. Thus, the United States economy is being bled dry. If illegal immigrants are allowed to stay on American soil, they will be lurking around the neighborhoods of average citizens, not the high security gated communities of our representatives and the self-appointed social justice warriors of Hollywood. Democracy? They decide things. You live with them. That is the current dispensation in this country. The majority decided, and their representation proceeds from the basis of what is described in the public narrative as a majority decision. However, that majority is in practice the lowest common denominator and the decision that is carried out appeals only to a limited number of people. Majority rule is a lie. Whether one is talking about Republicans or Democrats; Liberals or Conservatives,

Libertarians or Tea Partiers; everything is reduced to an image and the image is what is voted on. The People are then shocked when they realize that, far from the ideological platform or economic plan they had wanted, they have an image that talks; nothing more. That is how the politician-bureaucrat of the present age got his job. With so many of these politician-bureaucrats having started their political careers as lawyers and sophists, is it really surprising that our lawmakers know how to talk but not to carry out any kind of substantial action that will reform the system at its core? Besides, why would they want to reform a system that is none other than their bread and butter? Isn't it time you stopped investing your precious hope in all these lies and liars? One party represents political cronyism. The other represents economic cronyism. Both are up for sale. There is a growing number of people who look at both sides and then throw their votes away on lunatic fringe parties because they have despaired of all possible meaning for that vote.

Those who continue to vote demonstrate an almost inexhaustible faith in a system that they know from one election to the next will amount to a betrayal of their interests by the very candidate who claims to represent them, and yet the ballot boxes get filled every term. This phenomenon continues because if there is one thing party leadership is good at it is continuous salesmanship and marketing. Term after term the American voter is sold a lemon. He gleefully drives it off the lot and is surprised when the tires fall off. The American system in its current form represents 250 years of cunning, salesmanship, and chicanery coupled with the endless enthusiasm of Americans for a system they should know by now to be a disaster.

Not only is the electoral system a sham and a shambles; the economic system of our country is geared to produce happiness for the smallest amount of people while convincing the rest that this is what they wanted. The few enjoy paradise and are allowed to make day-to-day living a bone-crushing drudgery for the rest. What is truly alarming is how many

Americans are willing to attain to the top two percent and leave their countrymen to grind away in poverty and misery. The American dream is looking out for number one with no thought of anything beyond oneself. The early phases of the American dream allowed people to acquire a comfortable life through pluck and application. However, American capitalism ceased to be the system for the small business owner, the farmer, and tradesmen many decades ago. Shortly after the onslaught of the Industrial Revolution, American labor was stripped of its dignity and converted into a shapeless part of the shapeless mass that is the faceless proletariat. Large scale laissez fare capitalism, powered by its paymasters in the financial industry, no more serves the material needs and interests of the people in a true and substantive sense than globalism can serve the interests of individual Nations.

The masses may be easily beguiled, but individuals are not. When we speak with individual Americans, we encounter common sense, reason, and clear insight into the problems facing the nation. However, individuals are easily cowed, whether by brute force or simple starvation. It is the people as a unified force and behind a strong leader that corrupt governments and establishments truly fear. Any common citizen can be shown to be more mature, more developed, and less materialistic than any of their so-called representatives. What is needed therefore is more than just a movement. The people require an ideology that will make the best possible use of their best qualities. While this ideology may share certain features in common with what has gone before, we must not fail to understand that it acts against everything that has gone before, and seeks to give mankind a monopoly on its own future. This future ideology could best be characterized as a direct relationship between the people and their Leader. The instrumentality of government merely functions to bring about the unified designs of both.

The ideology to which I refer is taking shape here in America at this very moment and it is the work of many groups and many individuals working out the best possible pathway toward National Destiny. This ideology has elements of Fascism and Integralism. That last statement will terrify many. True to the old adage, people fear what they do not understand. People also fear what the PC propagandists demand they fear. Far from being understood, Fascism has been reviled and bastardized as a generic label for any behavior people view as rigid or any viewpoint that goes against the politically correct status quo. The generation of Americans that fought in World War II will have little positive to say about Fascism, unaware that Mussolini departed from his avowed Fascist doctrine very early in his career as Il Duce. Hitler never practiced Fascism. The National Socialist Party was an ideology composed of nationalism, socialism, and racism. General Franco of Spain began his career as Spain's Head of State (Caudillo) closely adhering to the principles of la Falange, the Spanish fascist party, but definitively drifted away from the doctrine laid down by Jose Antonio Primo de Rivera. The argument I just constructed will seem familiar to many; particularly to those who have fought against the old fallacy about true communism never having been practiced anywhere in the world. Fascism is the doctrine of the extreme middle, a third position, and the unified State making itself worthy of the utmost faith of its citizens.

If the 20th century was the century of the State, then it must be recognized that the State reached and surpassed its own peak of development, and is now everywhere in general decline. The original and legitimate function of statecraft is the manifestation of ideas, plans, and vision that are intended to achieve the greater good as well as the will of those who hold the reins of State. However no true vision or authority is remotely possible now, because states are fragmented, compartmentalized in a bizarre scheme of checks and balances that leaves every plan executed only partially and in a half-assed manner. Checks and balances, combined with the futile quibbling of partisan politics make it impossible for any true leadership to achieve little more than a fraction of its own designs. Arbitrary and convoluted, the modern State is a true product of modernity. It has no true Mission other than self-preservation.

The State must be united and organic. The electoral system is drawing on a gene pool that is more or less thinned out to an extreme. Americans believe they must sit by and watch as their interests are sidelined, marginalized, and betrayed by a professional political class whose laws of succession are based on heredity and money. This system continues for two primary reasons: One, it is a self-perpetuating autocracy suited to the needs of the political class that can best afford its privileges. Two, the people have lost the will to fight for what is truly theirs. Even when the Parties do manage enough altruism to make an attempt at genuine service of the People, their best intentions will inevitably give way to the endless vagaries of special interests and pocket-lining. While the State is run on partisan politics, the nation's trajectory will be a staggering zig zag reminiscent of the graphs and charts peppering the pages of the Wall Street Journal.

In order for the interests of the individual to be met by the Republicans or Democrats those interests must go through a general deformation. One disowns all that is not germane to the bottom line of capitalists. The other disowns all that is not part and parcel of that vague bogey: social justice. This has been going on for as long as this Republic has existed. With each election cycle the people expect less and less of their leaders, continue to put more and more faith in a system they know must ultimately fail them, and either feel betrayal when their candidate betrays their interests or exude a general attitude of death, dumb, and blind faith. The voters must play a game of make-believe, wherein they tell themselves their candidate has the power to achieve all good. When their candidate fails to deliver on his promises, they must tell the opposition that he is doing the best he can in view of the opposition he is getting from the other party. This is merely one fraction of the game.

The Integral State cannot allow for partisan politics or the bureaucratic aristocracy that has evolved in America today. The true state is the best, organic manifestation of the best qualities of the nation and its highest will. As such, it is an organism wherein roles are assigned to the cells that can best carry them out. Leadership is defined in the Integral State by talent and skill, not money and heredity. Let our leaders prove themselves

through their intelligence, their integrity, their presence, and the extent to

which they are ready, willing, and able to put their desires and inclinations

aside; to step outside of their petty, material egos and into that greater self

demanded of them by the Nation.

2.

THE MANIFESTO OF NATIONAL DESTINY

We firmly believe that human destiny is directed by a Great, Higher Intelligence and Power that frustrates all attempts at intellectual comprehension of it. A Supreme Being guides us. Humanity has throughout the eons struggled to emerge from chaos and, by the practice of virtues, to create order. Man's material skills serve mainly to ensure his continued existence. It is by dint of his less tangible, more refined skills that man strives to elevate his existence. All of man's skills and endowments exist for the promotion of well-being and happiness. It is only the perversion of these gifts and the subversion of the values that guide them that envelop the world in darkness. Man is called upon to live in harmony, to develop himself, and to care for the world in which he lives. To that end, every man has a vocation and a calling to follow. To do otherwise is to thwart that Grand Design by which this world and its life was made.

We hold certain truths to be self-evident; that human beings and the classes into which they are organized should live in harmony; that all have the power, the potential, the right, and the responsibility to develop their innate gifts for the betterment of themselves and their Nation; that States arise among men in order to best secure their lives, their property, and their way of life according to Law. The State must be united as an organic whole, ensuring the safety and harmony of its People, and commanding their respect in the utmost. The State must ensure that it is worthy of that respect, promoting leadership based solely on talent and loyalty regardless of social class, ethnicity, or material wealth. To that end the State must examine those citizens that would apply for positions of leadership, selecting only the most able and competent regardless of extraneous considerations and strenuously preventing the over-accumulation of wealth among its leaders.

We must allow for the organization of society into classes, recognizing that socioeconomic and political hierarchy is natural and desirable. Each citizen should enter into their class based on aptitude and skill. These classes must elect leadership from among their own for the best direction of their own interests and these leaders, in turn, must take part in municipal, regional, and state governance. These classes will form the syndicalized corporations that will shape economic as well as public policy. The classes will shape and discipline themselves as viable forces for the socioeconomic governance of the Nation. There must be harmony between these classes, for the Nation has need of discipline and order. Without these things there is not even the harmony enjoyed by denizens of the animal kingdom. There is only chaos and death without these things.

Let there be no mistaking this: That America is ruled de facto by the wealthy and the well-born. We have tragically allowed leadership to devolve into a lucrative, class-based vocation open only to a select few with the right friends and who can pay the very high price of admission. Indeed, this has been the pattern since democracy's earliest days. The city-state of ancient Greece and the Roman Republic were only democratic through very broad stretches of the imagination. Then as now, the privilege of representing the people (I am using the phrase ironically) was reserved for those who could pay for it. The closest thing that could be found to a man of the people in Rome was the Tribune chosen from the plebeian class. In the United States, our elected representatives have always been members of the privileged classes. George Washington was selected to lead the colonial army due to his experience in managing large numbers of people. The fact of the matter is that Washington owned the most slaves. Abraham Lincoln may have come from humble beginnings, but the man's political career would never have gotten off the ground had he not been a lawyer; part of the apparatus of hypocrisy. Why a Lincoln did indeed abolish slavery, he did nothing to establish true democracy. Neither did his predecessors nor his successors.

We do not seek a continuation of rule by the wealthy, nor do we seek a dictatorship of the proletariat. We prefer meritocracy, wherein leaders are chosen on the basis of their abilities proven through examination. The best possible leaders for this nation are out there right now, but they cannot

hold the reins of power while they are clutched in the hands of a moneyed

and over-privileged class. One extreme seeks to keep power in the hands of

a privileged class while the other seeks to redistribute all wealth and power

among an arbitrarily chosen cabal of protected classes. We seek to place the

leadership of this nation in the hands of those who are qualified through

integrity, intelligence, and dedication. Race is not a qualification. Sexual

preferences are not qualifications. Gender confusion is not a qualification.

Gender itself is not a qualification. Religion and Atheism are not

qualifications. The aforementioned list is made of qualities, not

qualifications. Those who would rule must demonstrate by their

intelligence, their aptitude, and their moral qualities but they are fit to do

so. Such a system must have the absolute support and loyalty of the

People. Indeed we seek to erect a system that will command the utmost

respect, support and loyalty of the people. Merely because such a system

has been thwarted every time an attempt has been made to create it does

not mean that it lacks a moral right to exist. Fascism and its sister ideology

Integralism have waited patiently in the wings. Now the future will take flight.

We confront the World head-on, taking it to be nothing less than an organic whole. We seek to build the society of the future, proceeding from the present one. That future society must be constructed on a hierarchy of values. This hierarchy is based on the principle of authority as a sacred manifestation (*auctoritas*), and ensures the primacy of the Divine over the National, and the National over the Regional, the Regional over the Local, and the Local as the best manifestation of the unity of individuals, families, and communities in joint effort with corporative syndicates. This authority to which I refer is the principal unifying force ensuring the convergence of social forces, the harmonious operation of those forces in cooperation with those of the State. The State shall serve to harness the powers of the Nation to its highest good. This is the greatest opportunity any group of human beings has ever been given, for if we do not push the State and society to their highest good then these shall fall into a chaos that will hold sway for decades if not centuries.

The Nation is a great, unified society of families, communities, corporative interests, values, racial and cultural identity. Like the State, it is a unified, organic entity. Otherwise, it is fragmented and dying. A country that has long made it a practice of admitting members of all races and cultures irrespective of values will inevitably tear itself apart. The die has been cast. America is a country of many races and cultures. However, this does not preclude the possibility of transforming it into an organic and integral whole: a Nation in the truest sense. Values must be shared and enforced. Education must be reformed and changed into a vehicle for the inculcation of knowledge and character, not the systematic subversion of values. Through education and training we will erect a nation of workers and clear thinkers devoted to a common cause. That common cause is nothing less than National Destiny.

Once the essential character of Nationhood is grasped, it being inseparable from a good and proper model of citizenship, the State can be constructed on three fundamental principles: natural hierarchy, social harmony, and the highest, common good. Natural hierarchy recognizes a natural tendency for human society to be structured, not based on fictive, 18th century bourgeois notions of equality, but according to the strengths and weaknesses that inherently exist in human beings and which it is unhealthy and perilous to ignore. Social harmony emphasizes that a hierarchical society need not be at war with itself, for each has skills, merits, and a place among his peers. Classes, trades, professions, ethnic and cultural groups all have functions to perform, each to the benefit of the others. Our highest, common good is National Destiny, wherein the integral whole achieves the pinnacle of spiritual, social, cultural, and economic well-being.

The custodian of National Destiny is the State, which must assume responsibility for the legitimate aspirations of the People. We proclaim in full the Rights of Man, insisting that human liberty be conjoined with human responsibility. Not only do the People have the responsibility to obey the Law and the State, but also to exert full effort to develop themselves. Let each become all he is capable of being, and let the State, in cooperation with the People's corporations, erect structures for the support of this development.

As for our leaders (both the leaders of this movement and the leaders of the future state), let them take heed that the age of indolent plutocracy is over. Those who lead the nation shall have a living; a salary appropriate to the work they do, nothing more. The age of inherited power is over. This country can ill afford more corrupt dynasties with names such as Kennedy and Bush; names that have come to the associated with luxury and entitlement in a country where most of the people live in poverty and powerlessness. Leadership is earned buy effort and personal qualities, not by birth and money. Our leaders must be exemplars of excellence, not wealthy pigs. If they will not submit to regular examinations to prove their intelligence and aptitude; if they will not subject themselves to testing in order to prove their integrity, they must be removed. The Declaration of Independence clearly states that when any government becomes destructive of the ends for which it was constructed (eg, life, liberty, and the pursuit of happiness) it is the right of the people to dismantle and replace it. After all, those who possess integrity do not object if it is tested.

We envision the state as an essentially populist, authoritarian organism. We believe that the state has the sovereignty, the authority, and the duty to manifest the will of the nation. This state must also act as society's guiding force, coordinating the forces of society's natural structures. As we design the integral, fascist state, we cannot go wrong. To begin with, we shall be dismantling a superstructure that is past corruption and decadence. Furthermore, in doing so we shall be mindful of the same imperatives driving us has move this new society forward: Namely, natural hierarchy, social harmony, and National Destiny. As we proceed with this architecture, we will step out of our selves and into the new, transcendental roles decreed for us by this National Destiny.

For us, the family is the nuclear unit of society. Its nature is biological and spiritual, having the duty of nurturing the body, mind, and soul of the individual. All human life begins in the family. The most important and honorable traditions of mankind are kept safe in the Repository of family life. We seek to erect a state that will stop at nothing to preserve the Integrity of the family against all forces that seek to subvert it. We wish to promote the family as the most basic training ground of respect, strength, honor, as well as the principal virtues. We wish to defend the family as a communion of hearts and Minds. The family is the womb of society. Most hitherto existing legislation add salt to a road the basic foundations of the family. We consider it one of our highest priorities to nurture the family, to provide the best Integral and traditional education for children, and we also seek to inculcate those personal qualities that will best allow the child to advance in life.

Since the family is so vital to the society and State we wish to build, we think it is right set a family wage be maintained in the economy. Parents should not have to choose between the children they love and the jobs they need. We also seek to address the ailments of the family on the social level. The high rate of divorce does not merely point to a crisis in the institution of marriage, but in the social structures that are intended to support it. Decline of morality, the rise of sex as nearly a spectator sport, the intrusion of public into private life and vice versa, are only a few of the social and political ailments laying siege to the family. Therefore let our enemies take note: We fully intend to integrate the family into our program to reconstruct society and the state. We intend to restore the family to its privileged position as the foundational element of civilization, and our cadres welcome all resistance because light can only be seen as light when it overcomes the darkness.

We further intend to reform education more or less completely. Our children are emerging from the education system confused about matters pertaining to sex and private life, they are overwhelmed with information hurled at them by institutions that can no longer discern essential from nonessential knowledge, and many of them are entering into Collegiate education with minimal reading comprehension and writing skills. As to their knowledge of History, find American history in particular, they are given only those elements that will support the political agenda of the unions and pay masters of their teachers (and I use the term teachers very lightly). They have no sense of Destiny because they have not been given a sense of History. There has been nearly 150 years of debate concerning whether or not history is even a relevant subject. It is relevant to every man, as it is the fundamental account of our heritage. Scholars have argued endlessly for and against the concept of historicism and the historical sense. History is there. It happened. We owe a debt to the Past. History will be taught in our schools.

We seek to eradicate the Common Core and all such systems aiming at the dumbing down of the Nation. We aim to restore teaching of the Arts and literature. We seek the mandatory teaching of American history devoid of revisionism. We shall uphold standards for teachers whereby the math teacher is required to have a broad knowledge of mathematics. The history teacher is required to know history. The English teacher is required to know the mechanics of the English language and English literature. Their methods do not concern us. What does concern us is that they be knowledgeable and trustworthy. Teachers are grilled concerning all manner of standardized systems and useless policies. Meanwhile, our children are not even aware that, prior to the 18th century we were a colony of the British Empire. Meanwhile, 12 year old girls heart being impregnated. Meanwhile, teachers are molesting and raping their students. The priorities of American Education are standardized systems, contract negotiations, and strikes. Not to worry. We shall reform the teaching profession in full.

Another of our aims is supervision of the state over the Arts and the humanities. We shall bring to an end the era wherein enormous grant monies subsidized by the taxpayers shall be awarded two artists specializing in obscenity and disrespect for our basic institutions. We do not seek to squash creativity. We seek to reform it. Every citizen shall be entitled to their viewpoint, but under our Direction the age of Hollywood celebrities posing as political pundits shall come to a close. Furthermore, the journalistic media no longer cloak its ulterior motives beneath the nebulous enablement of "freedom of the press". The peddling of narratives designed to move a specific agenda forward and disguising as news will be dealt with. It must be stopped. The only legitimate partnership in the forming of opinions is between the people and the State.

We aim to promote the moral and Spiritual Development of this nation. We declare war on materialism. We seek to create a society unhindered by liberalism as it tries to subvert all the vital forces of the nation. We harbor nothing but respect for a free conscience, country will guarantee freedom of religion, criminal prosecution for those deemed overly litigious against religious institutions, criminal prosecution for any and all religious leaders who abuse children and animals in any way, and criminal prosecution for those who use their religion for their lack of it as a means to threaten the peace and social harmony of this nation for the well-being of its citizens.

We believe in a Supreme Being, although we leave it to the individual to contemplate the specific characteristics of the Supreme Being. We do not accept the atheist because he is not content merely to not believe. The atheist will not feel secure until atheism has been enforced everywhere. In psychology this is called paranoid megalomania. We believe in a god and the subject ends there.

The state shall direct the national economy, encouraging private ownership and private Enterprise while discouraging mass capitalism laissez faire, and declaring war on the cult of materialist consumerism. The legitimate forces of production shall not be inhibited, and the principles of supply and demand Shelby subjugated to the needs of the people. We shall not subject

ourselves to a plutocracy; a government of the wealthy, by the wealthy,

and for the wealthy. We shall do all in our power to curb the economic

sovereignty of bourgeois capitalism, the subversion of legitimate economic

forces buy communist socialist operatives, we shall ensure prosperity but

not greed and luxury for the people. We uphold the right of property

owners subject to the common good. We acknowledge that private

enterprise creates prosperity while upholding a belief that certain

industries must belong exclusively to the Nation. Banking, transportation

and energy production are two such Industries that must be nationalized.

These must not be exploited for profit because their sole purpose is the

development of the national economy and the public interest.

We uphold all these games and more. We are fascists because we believe in

the Primacy of the State and its unification under one purpose and one

Leader toward National Destiny. We are Integralist, seeking the efficient

and beneficent operation of the State as a holistic organism and social harmony, economic prosperity, and True Justice. We invite you to stand

with us. Abiding by the highest principles, standing together in true

Brotherhood, with strength and honor, we will Triumph.

3.

LIBERALISM

Before beginning this chapter, I would like to say a word on pronoun usage. With the emergence of the Left's newest psychosis, that of gender identity politics, there is a new delusion that a human being can become an epicene. For the unfamiliar, an epicene is a third-person pronoun that can refer to plural antecedents of any gender and, under certain circumstances, to a singular antecedent that refers to a male or female (but not inanimate) entity. Words such as "they" come to mind. Since it is now fashionable among Liberals to avoid all references to gender-specific pronouns, I will throughout this chapter and, hopefully, this book, with a term as neutral as I could find. It seems to me that the word "it" would be most applicable. I feel certain most of my readers will agree.

Liberalism seeks to open the subject of National Destiny to free debate, as if it does not matter whether the Nation thrives or dies. Indeed, Liberalism is so weak-willed and pernicious that it cannot stomach the concept of duality, and so it attempts to eradicate all differences of every kind. Liberals live in the hope that, if they can manage to remove value from the equation, then everything will be equally worthless and interchangeable. Thus, National Destiny is no different for them than the contents of a sheep's bladder. After all, if everything is equally worthless, then National Destiny is no different than a sheep's bladder.

However, this is not truly how the Liberal thinks and operates. The Liberal does uphold a sense of value, albeit strictly extrinsic, utilitarian, and mercenary. Nothing is valuable in and of itself for the Liberal, even if its mouth forms the words, "That's not true". The Liberal's value system is surgically trimmed, altered, and tailored to fit whatever agenda it has at that particular moment. If today's fad is transgendered bathroom usage, then the Liberal will ardently and viciously insist that the dichotomy of gender is nothing more than a construct employed by the Patriarchy in order to suppress the multitudes, all of whom desire to change genders from day to day as if they were trying on shoes. This is especially true if there is Federal money available to combat the currently popular "social problem". The values the Liberal does accept are grafted and removed from its body politic so often that they lose all integrity. Nothing has its original shape. Everything becomes as the Liberal wanted it; a shapeless mass. In the end, the Liberal value system is repugnant and repellant to anyone with a shred of integrity in them due to this very process of grafts and attachments. The Liberal is a true Dr. Frankenstein, proposing to liberate men but creating a hideous monster.

The Liberal desires strife between all parties, provided its own party is always perceived as the victor. I say *perceived* as the victor, for it must be remembered that no intrinsic value can be posited for the Liberal and what it desires. Indeed, the last thing it wants is to be locked in, tied to, or committed to a solid system of value. The Liberal prefers its values be plastic, interchangeable with everything else, and well within the guidelines for Federal funding. There is no reality. There is only what is perceived. This is, of course, the natural outcome of that relativism that is as close as the Liberal will ever get to a true core value. The strife is essential to the Liberal program, because no Liberal can stomach or summon the character to rule over a Nation united under one purpose. That is because one of the Liberal's basic facts is that social decay and disorder are the most desirable traits, for they ensure the perceived need for social workers, freelance crusaders, and self-appointed "social justice warriors" always ready to be on the receiving end of taxpayer monies the government has been assured are vitally necessary to prevent that social collapse that, in the Liberal's narrative, is always imminent. The Liberal also cannot stomach the social and moral order a unified Nation would impose. To begin with, this would amount to a large portion of social workers and the self-appointed being out of a job. The last thing a social worker wants is for the inner city black, single mother to stop using drugs, stop drinking and smoking, and take night classes in order to complete her education and obtain a better position. No social problems means no social programs and no social workers. For the Liberal nothing but public disorder, moral decay, and continuous entropy are to be sought.

The Liberal State is a nightmare or nihilism, near anarchy, and nearly total entropy. This is because the Liberal believes in nothing but whatever will suit its current purposes, and these are subject to change based on trends enforced by popular demand and desire, themselves motivated by the whims of media, consumerism, and the latest left-wing madness seeping out of those pestilential sinkholes that have the temerity to call themselves centers of learning. As for the Liberal State, it is quite capable and liable to suspend civil liberty whenever the occasion seems to demand it, for the Liberal does not believe in the liberty or sovereignty of the People. The Liberal believes in nothing but its own perceived benefit and pleasure, and this is what enables it to so easily exchange this value for that at a moment's notice. It is not above suspending the very Law of the land in order to achieve what it wants. Even the dual nature of the biological organism; the fact that there are only *two* genders and these are a matter of birth and biology, can come under attack if the Liberal feels it will benefit by doing so. Let us not lose sight of the fact that Liberalism is the bastard child of Marx's dialectical materialism, which supports the criminalization of whichever sciences contradict its dictates. I will elaborate on this in a later chapter.

The Liberals of our current day and age are a far cry from those that fought in the Spanish Civil War. The Liberals of 80 years ago at least had the virtue of believing in core principles of decent human conduct, even in combat. Today's Liberal is a violent, loud-mouthed, disrespectful savage who will stoop to any depth in order to get what it wants. I direct the reader's attention to the "Occupy" movement of 2011. My original intent had been to present a complete list of crimes and bestial atrocities committed by the minions of that despicable eddy of filth. However, when that list grew to a number greater than 400, I choked back my bile and contented myself to presenting only a portion of all the crimes for which the Occupiers should be shot. The list follows:

- Madison, WI: 10-27-2011 — Madison Occupiers lose their permit due to public masturbation.

- Phoenix, AZ: 10/28/2011 — Flier handed out at Occupy Phoenix asks, "When Should You Shoot a Cop?"
- Cleveland, OH: 10/18/2011 — 'Occupy Cleveland' Protester reports she was raped.
- Seattle, WA: 10/18/2011 – Protester arrested for exposing himself to children.
- Portland, OR: 10/16/2011 — Protester desecrates memorial To U.S. War Dead.
- New York: 10/25/2011 — Three protesters threatened to kill woman for reporting rape by one of their friends.
- Oakland, CA: 10/24/2011 — Protesters storm, vandalize, and shut down Chase Bank.
- Boston, MA: 10/23/2011 — Occupy Boston Protesters arrested for dealing heroin in a tent while a 6-year old child was present.
- New Orleans, LA: 11/8/2011 — Man dead for two days found in Occupy encampment.

The list could be much longer, but could easily take us too far afield of our theme. I just wish to point out, before moving on, that rape seems to have been among the favorite crimes of the Occupiers. Also, I should point out that Neo-Nazis threw their lot in with this movement, which only helps to further demarcate Fascism from Nazism. We are not allies of Wall Street, nor are we proponents of public disorder and anarcho-hedonism, which is all this movement achieved, and that as nothing more than a momentary "burp" in the American consciousness. Now the "movement" is dead. Good riddance.

The Liberal speaks of rights for all. It speaks of universal liberty and unrestrained freedom. However, even a three-minute discussion with one will reveal to even the crudest thinker that the Liberal's real intent is as far from liberty as anyone could conceive. The Liberal craves freedom, liberty, and opportunity as it dictates for those who agree with its agenda. For the rest there shall be marginalization, ostracism, and unending persecution. All this is in line with that unending browbeating that passes for most of the Liberal's true methodology. The finger that liberals have traditionally pointed at Fascism is on the very hand that beats down on the very people Liberals claim to champion.

How did Liberalism go from the partisans of 80 years ago to the jar-shitting, unwashed rapists of the Occupy movement and their luminaries? The answer is quite simple. The Liberals of 80 years ago and today both adhere to subversion as a primary goal. This subversion is disguised as liberation. Subversion is negation, and negation is applied in the liberal project to every value that supports what is thought of as the old order.

The only thing that can replace an old order is new social, political, and moral chaos. Thus, once liberals have achieved their State, and there is nothing more for them to do, they continue the process of subversion. They cannot stop the ravening beast. All values are eventually subverted by the Liberal, and the revolutionary pistol is eventually pointed at itself. As an old saying goes, it's an ill bird that fouls its own nest.

The Liberal cannot and will not stand up in debate. The Liberal outwardly considers debate with its opponent ridiculous; all the while inwardly cringing at the prospect of an argument that cannot be manipulated to degenerate into an emotional, insulting shouting match. The Liberal shrinks from real arguments and argumentation because these processes are grounded in fact. To the non-critical thinker and the Liberal, facts are tedious, and they require a decent familiarity with the subject under discussion. Finally, any Liberal with half a brain (and it only requires half a brain to be a Liberal in the first place) would cease to be a liberal and at the very least become a moderate once any degree of factual knowledge is acquired. This is why Liberal polemics are so furious and bile-driven.

Liberal bile is a narcotic that dulls the senses and the mind, so that all

presumptions at making an argument are replaced with feeling-based

ranting, which is fine for speech making and demagogy, but it has no place

in rational discourse and debate. Truth be told, for all its attempts at

negating truth and belief, the Liberal embraces its opinions as others accept

religious revelation. This makes rational debate with the Liberal

impossible. The only option is to fight, and the only way to fight an

ideological war is to construct the Right Ideology, and not Right referring

to the traditional sense that emerged in the National Assembly in France,

but Right as in "correct".

It is my intent in this book to provide key ideas toward the basis of just

such an ideology. I will begin with a series of thoughts, themselves all

leading in the same direction but each from a different point. My intent in

the next chapter is to provide my reader with a series of "seed-thoughts" as

it were, for his contemplation.

4.

PRINCIPLES OF COMMUNITY ACTION

- The force that will lead mankind forward from darkness to light is Fascism. It is imperative that we win the confidence of the People, for Fascism is Unity. If we do not stand arm-in-arm with the people; if we do not work alongside them, we neither earn nor deserve Power, and never doubt for a moment that the People are Power.

- Visit the sick, feed the poor, and assist the elderly. Be a mentor to the young and help the afflicted to recover their dignity. Do not wait for the People to ask for our help; offer it. People are very proud, and they are sometimes unwilling or unable to ask for help. If we help them and preserve their pride, they will stand and fight for our Cause.

- Victory will belong to whoever serves the People. Service and defense of the People is the way to victory. It is a simple matter of numbers. The People are far more numerous than any elite minority that rules over them. Therefore, it is always in the best interests of those who would rule to gain the intimate trust of the People. Know what matters to them. Care about what they care about. Then you will see what needs to be done.

- The Rulers of the Future State will rise from this Fascist movement. It must be emphasized again and again that our first order of business must be to win over the hearts and minds of the People. Where else do any of us come from?

- You must know the minds of the People. To know the minds of the People, you must listen to them. However, in order to truly hear the People you must first get your own cleverness out of your ears. Listen and learn from the People and in time they will line up to hear you.

- The People are our ideological battlefield. We must not surrender so much as an inch!

- Each of us must become the change we want to see in society. Therefore, do the right thing because it is the right thing to do. Follow the Code.

- Maintaining high morale as well as high morals in the face of the drudgeries, corruptions, and decadence of the world will forge you into a weapon of steel. If the Party is to become the Future State, we shall need many such weapons.

- Life is strength. To despair of the struggle is decay and death. If we truly live we will inevitably have an effect upon the world. We truly live when we acknowledge the struggle that lives in us. Man can only become what is best in him through struggle. Make no mistake: ours is a revolutionary struggle, though its character is essentially a reaction.

- Do not lose heart! Our reactive revolution comprises far more than the problems of the hour and fads of our time! The Fascist Vision encompasses, better than any other ideology, the cosmic perspective. That is why you must study and meditate on the great cycles of history, life, and time. You must expand your sight! You must come to recognize that, to your perspective it shall seem as if nothing ever changes but the minutiae. In truth, every moment of your struggle is a shovelful of dirt on the graves of our enemies, the greatest of which is materialism. Rejoice!

- Though we shall engage the enemy in bitter struggle, it is what we do in peace that will determine victory or defeat. Read! Study! Know what we struggle for! Strengthen yourself in body, mind, and spirit each day! Keep the mind sharp and clear, like a diamond sword. Keep narcotics out of your body. Do not drink to drunkenness. Avoid tobacco. Avoid pornography and prostitution in any form. We need you to make of yourself a great and shining force!

- To be better than our enemies, you must avoid telling yourself that you are better than our enemies. You must struggle each day to become better. Spiritually, morally, mentally, and physically you must struggle to become better than you were the day before. Remember that Fascism has always characterized itself as a Workers' movement. We must work on ourselves daily or we are defeated.

- Everything that is worth doing is worth doing well. We are not content with mediocrity. That dreadful sleep is why our Nation's children have degenerated into idiots who are left behind in mathematics, science, technology and industry by countries like Singapore. We have become lazy. We have become happier with mediocrity. We have abandoned that struggle that is the human heritage. The only solution is to cultivate less self-satisfaction and more self-discipline. It is that simple.

- It is through you; the individual Fascist, that we shall make the People aware of their own power. This will be accomplished through the path of daily struggle. You must push yourself to grow and develop every day. You must, as Nietzsche said, discover ten truths a day. If not ten truths, then climb ten mountains! Conquer ten worlds! Leave your doubts in the void and act on the heroic impulse!

- As we ascend to the Future State, we shall have many occasions to hunt down and expose the deeds of our enemies. Greedy capitalists, professional politicians, self-satisfied bureaucrats, liberals, communists, paparazzi, and materialists in general must be exposed in the light of this Great Movement.

- You are Fascism. It lives and breathes in you. Be aware of this and govern your conduct accordingly. You, the individual cadre, are our missionary and ambassador. You are the foundation of the Future State. You must therefore purge yourself of the toxins of materialism and heresy.

5.

ANTIMATERIALISM

The beating heart of Fascism is its uncompromising stance against materialism. We reject all notions and systems that require a view of mankind as a plasticized material object whose sole substance is substance itself. We reject the capitalist view which savagely seeks to pigeon-hole humanity as a producer, a consumer, or a corpse. We reject the communist/Marxist view which upholds that humanity can only be happy while being deprived of the fundamental rights of property, self-expression, and which sees people as either statistics or cannon-fodder. All materialist views of the human being are violence against human beings, stripping them of their essential dignity and reducing them to substance. We will direct our violence toward all such views and, when necessary, the proponents of such views.

Why are we so vehement in our opposition to materialism? The plain and simple fact is that the human *being* is not *substance*. Any other position is immoral and dangerous. Though we may live in bodies and act through bodies, it can only be accepted and not denied that the body is the agent, not the essence, of the human being. This will never change no matter how repugnant it may be to the ignorant and the wicked. The human being possesses an essence that defines who he is and distinguishes him from all the rest of creation. This is the first and final fact of human nature, and will remain so regardless of our acceptance or rejection. To do otherwise among States is to create a society of depravity and deprivation.

This depraved, deprived social condition is one way the materialists (represented politically/economically by the Capitalists and Communists) have kept the People under their thumbs. When you deny that an animal is a thinking, feeling, sentient being, it has nowhere to go but the slaughterhouse. When human beings are denied their essential humanity, they become objects and substance and it is far easier to perpetuate perpetual atrocities upon them. Only the grossest self-deception contorts this situation in order to impute to it some sort of humane agenda. We seek

to defend humanity from those who would pulverize it in order to justify

some perverted view of themselves as the super-golden this or social

justice warrior of that. We shall do so with extreme prejudice.

The Capitalist wants to reduce all men to producers and consumers. In

order to increase his profits, he will lower costs by shipping jobs to foreign

markets where he can get away with paying far lower wages. This

increases unemployment, which forces the State to borrow more money

from the finance capitalists in order to subsidize welfare and ensure that

buying power remains the same. The production capitalist and the finance

capitalist, through the pipeline of the State, are allowed to effectively

squeeze everything they can out of society and, when that fruit is reduced

to a husk, they are allowed to cast their victims aside and seek new prey.

Production should serve society's needs and we question the need of an

elite few to draw an annual income in the billions while there are people

who, despite their best efforts, are unable to feed, clothe, or shelter

themselves. Like the socialist, we deplore exploitation of the laboring masses. However, the socialist seeks to reduce all to the lowest common denominator; a grinding poverty controlled tightly by the state where citizens are pigeon-holed, taxed, and transplanted from the machinery of the factory to the machinery of the State. There is far more to human beings than the latest fashions and toys; the latest "social justice" program. There is far more to us than our ability to prop up the establishment and be as mere cogs in the great, ungodly machines of the capitalists and socialists. Capitalism and Communism share materialism in common. The belief that progress is measured by an abundance of things and that the ultimate goal in life is to be the most powerful pig in the slaughterhouse is a complete error in thinking that Fascism seeks to correct by restoring to Man his proper dignity and nobility. We aim to create a society where success is measured in terms of pride and dignity and the fulfillment of needs is never in doubt.

6.

MARXIST MATERIALISM

We begin our attack on materialism with an attack on its Marxist or Marxian prong, which attempts to view all of history solely in economic terms and in terms of class struggle, which Marx would have us believe are one in the same. By reducing society to economic classes, Marxists believe they have succeeded in the first steps of their revolution. However, reduction to absolute materialism in the Marxian scheme can only function by some of the most grotesque perversions of thought known to man. They are grotesque in their subtlety and in the harm they have wrought in societies unfortunate enough to have had them applied. Communism collapsed in Russia in 1990. Decades have passed and Russian society is still dealing with the harms wrought by Leninist/Stalinist depravity. Let us be clear on Marx's misreading of the social phenomenon of class.

Few would fail to recognize the role of classes in political and social life. However, Marxists and those in process of falling victim to that contagion assume that economics (no matter how economic classes are defined) always has an overriding significance in relation to other social drives-- religious, national, racial, or sexual. This is, in part the essence of Marxist materialism and it is every bit as mistaken as Mao's belief that grain farmers were qualified to produce steel in their backyards. There is also a mistaken belief in the universality of class antagonism, which would imply that the Proletariat in toto was opposed to World War 1. It was clearly to the interests of the working classes in all countries to oppose the First World War. Many political parties and movements that garnered the support of the working class had pledged themselves to oppose military solutions before the war broke out. However, once war had been declared the bulk of the working classes rallied to the support of their respective governments with no less patriotism than that exhibited by their counterparts.

This belief in economic override leads to the preposition that technological advances in modes of production inevitably lead to changes in the social relations of production. This is absurd as saying that the introduction of

mechanized production was responsible for the rise of unions. Marxism

upholds the belief that the economic 'base' of society supports, is reflected

by and influences an ideological 'superstructure' which encompasses

culture, religion, politics, and all other aspects of humanity's social

consciousness, thus reducing all of human history to a bit of effluvium. It

thus looks for the causes of developments and changes in human history in

economic, technological, and more broadly, material factors, as well as the

clashes of material interests among tribes, social classes, and nations. Law,

politics, the arts, literature, morality, religion – are understood by Marx to

make up the 'superstructure', as reflections of the economic base of society.

Usage of the term "class" in Marxist literature is multifarious. Not all uses

are consistent with each other, even if they are valid. Sometimes "class"

indicates a group's role in production. Another use of the term derives

from the common mode of life, culture and traditions of a social group.

"Class" can also indicate the source or level of a social group's income. It

can point to a social group's economic position as having or not having a vocation. In the Communist Manifesto Marx shrieks that "all history is the history of class struggles". No genuine Marxist is unaware of this maxim. However, not a single class struggle has been economic in any of the above senses, and Marxists are always insistent that the economic sense overrides all, thus embracing a self-refuting ideology, which is most impressively absurd in a surrealist, street performer sense. History most decidedly is not entirely the history of class struggles. Certainly, one can choose to view history in this manner. One can also dose heavily on LSD and choose to view all of history as any variety of hallucinations.

History contains far more evidence of class cooperation and apathy than class struggle. Certainly, the working and middle classes always harbor some degree of resentment toward the rich. However, we are not addressing the history of class resentment because resentment, no matter how much Occupy Wall Street insisted on it, is not struggle. For a theory to be accepted as a law it must be demonstrated through empirical evidence, which Marx's dialectical materialism decries on the basis that it refutes dialectical materialism. For evidence I invite the reader to do his own research into sciences that were banned in the Soviet Union because their findings opposed Marx's delusions. The list includes biology, physics, history, sociology, and a few others. The "law of class struggle" either cannot be a law because it has so many exceptions or it is applicable in so few actual cases as to be totally irrelevant.

It is not only the Marxist concept of class struggle that is illegitimate; the uncritical extension of the class struggle into all areas of human experience is as well. The practice among self-identified Marxists is to restructure cultural, religious, and intellectual conflicts as well as scientific development as corollaries of a struggle for a greater share of social wealth and power, not for the Proletariat, but for the small, Marxist elite that always emerges in any country where left-wing agitation is carried to its virulent extreme. It robs the traditional monarchies of their divine right; the owner of capital of his ownership, and then presumes to euphemistically liberate the masses. However, this liberation is absolute tyranny with divine and proprietary rights replaced with the Marxist mumbo-jumbo of "historical inevitability".

Marx's refuted theory of historical materialism cannot explain the transition from feudalism to capitalism. Feudal societies have existed in many periods and regions of the world, but capitalism arose in Europe, not all over the globe as Marx and Marxists insist. Capitalism spread to many parts of the world, but not because of any immanent law of the development of the social relations in feudalism but because it was brought to other parts of the world, as import or export. There is even less evidence to support the universality of the transition from slave to feudal societies. Such transitions can fit into Marx's account of history only after one has ignored all other facts. Modern anthropology, also on the Soviet blacklist of sciences, has long provided conclusive evidence refuting Marx's account of primitive societies, and we will not go into the evidence here as it can readily be found in any library by the most cursory perusal of basic textbooks on the subject.

Even for the period of capitalism, Marx's theory of historical materialism is inadequate. Historical materialism seeks to explain all major political and cultural changes in terms of the development in the mode of economic production. This would imply that Henry Ford's innovations that led to assembly line production in the automobile industry were directly responsible for the Coolidge Administration's lack of decisive action during the Great Mississippi Flood of 1927. It is utter nonsense and fallacious thinking at best. Such a sweeping claim cannot be established except on a statistical basis, which is ironic in view of historical or dialectical materialism's refutation of statistics as a valid science. Marx ignores the fact that the economic basis of society at any given time is often compatible with more than one political form. Production takes place even when a government collapses completely into dysfunction, as is the case with the disastrously limited production of consumer goods in North Korea. A nation's political structures are attributable to far more than the predominant modes of production. Only the laziest or most delusional

thinker would posit otherwise.

Apologists state that Marxism does not claim that the economic base of

society is the only social determinant. In a letter written by Friedrich

Engels, Marx's long-time sugar-daddy, we read:

> According to the materialist conception of history, the ultimately determining
> element in history is the production and reproduction of real life. More than this
> neither Marx nor I ever asserted. Hence if somebody twists this into saying that
> the economic element is the only determining one he transforms that proposition
> into a meaningless, abstract, senseless phrase.

However, this is more corner painting. If the superstructure influences the

base then Marx's constant assertions that the history of society is one of

economic class conflict is moot. It leads directly into pointless questions of

causality. Apologists try to alleviate this by saying that Marx viewed

economics as the ultimate reality. According to Marx, humanity's defining

characteristic was its means of production. Therefore, man can only be

freed from oppression by seizing control of the means of production. This is the Marxists teleology and the elements of the superstructure are its causal conditions.

The critique of Marxism and Marxian socialism can occupy volumes. However, such an exhaustive study is not the purview of this book. My purpose is to outline symptoms of the spiritual disease currently destroying the West and to provide a cure. Marxism and Marxian socialism form one half of the symptom of materialism. The other half of the symptom is provided by Capitalism.

7.

CAPITALIST MATERIALISM

Nothing indicates the alienation of politics in the present day than the fact that capitalism is effectively off-limits to critical review or discussion. When it is permissible for capitalism to be mentioned by politicians or pundits, it is with reverential tones worthy of a religious devotee. They are devoted to the spirit of the marketplace, where nothing less than human flesh is the prime unit of exchange and the human soul is the price of admission. Even more insidious is the fact that large scale bourgeois capitalism, vital to the production of products to fulfill human needs, has been hijacked. It has been intimately linked to private ownership and the intended dream of private ownership where each individual was deemed worthy to and entitled to carry out his own economic freedom has been aborted.

Worst of all: Capitalism has reduced modern Man to less than an animal. He is part statistic, part machine, all material. Humans are fed into the machinery of production like so much fuel and lubricant. They are machine parts to be used up and thrown away, but not before buying and consuming as much product as they possibly can. To be sure, the Worker will not be able to afford much of what he produces, but he is required to maintain faith in the process and the product or rather the availability of the product. He is not permitted to relinquish belief that, one day, he may be able to own what he produces. That he may one day own or control the means of production has never been at issue in capitalism. Through systematically alienating the Worker, Bourgeois capitalism has managed to produce Labor that can barely conceive owning or controlling what it produces, much less the means of production.

Books have been written, and more should be written, concerning the history of production as an economic, social, and technological phenomenon. One has undeniably influenced and conditioned the other.

Modern production has brought with it the development of capital and the mutually conditioning proletarian/bourgeois classes. It has also brought with it the most insidious product of alienation: mass marketing and consumerism. 21st Century Capitalism is nearly inseparable from mass marketing, itself inseparable from mass production. Branding is the inseparability of product, producer, and advertiser. Brands are pushed in mass media as elements of identity. The mass media sells identities as surely as the black market specializes in stolen ID's. The net result is the popular cult of Consumerism, which is the new opiate of the masses and has replaced the religious quest for self-realization with the materialistic scramble for self-branding.

In capitalist dysfunction, personal identity is a commodity to be manufactured, moved, processed, and purchased. The process functions in much the same manner as the Inquisition of the Middle Ages. The individual's identity is harshly and immoderately critiqued, analyzed, and judged to be inadequate. This is done with the same ruthlessness as a

Maoist struggle session. The individual is urged to relinquish their previously existing identity in favor of the new, manufactured identity. This new identity is marketed as a "lifestyle" comprising "appropriate" (manufacturer and advertiser approved) choices in fashion, music, food, entertainment, technology and other products. This new conception of identity arises from a basic delusion, fed into by sociologists, psychologists, journalists, artists, and Reality TV, that individuals can effectively alter their identity merely by altering their patterns of consumption. In other words, we become what we consume.

The great irony here is that, due to the rise of globalism, many global brands are not things-in-themselves. Manufacturing, material processing, packaging, and marketing are all outsourced to countries where labor is cheap, further testifying that the so-called "global age" with its political correctness and emphasis on socialistic redistribution schemes is every bit as imperialistic as Marx accused Bourgeois Capitalists of becoming in the later stages of Capitalism. The brands to which consumers turn for the construction of their intensely-craved false identities are not even the objects the consumers imagine them to be, but are instead product surrogates having nothing to do with the brightly-colored idol presented on the TV screen or color supplement. Companies are no longer truly in the business of producing things. Rather, they are in the business of producing the image of their product. The image, and not the product, is what is being consumed.

The formula of Capitalism has remained unchanged since the days of the Industrial Revolution. A manufacturer or merchant will always seek to maximize profit and minimize loss. Hence, the very lucrative practices of modern consumer capitalism have resulted in streamlined companies competing to produce the most powerful images, not products, and gaining the largest, most dynamic portions of the ever-expanding market share. Less and less actual product trickles down to the masses. Instead, what is purveyed is an idolatrous image and a cult of image control.

Nowhere is this more apparent than the rituals of Reality TV makeover and real estate shows.

The American "make-over" show always features a bevy of underpaid, underskilled, underdeveloped (intellectually, morally, spiritually) women who are then brought to shame or even tears for not cultivating the "proper" or "fashionable" image. They are mocked, humiliated, shamed, and the disciplined into embracing the new image identity. They are then encouraged to "sell" this identity to the modern, image- and identity-obsessed materialistic world at large in an act that is adequately termed by marketing experts as "self-branding": a term that brings to mind imagery associated with the rituals of the cattle ranch. Real Estate makeover shows are little different; associating success in obtaining an "acceptable" or "fashionable" domicile of one's "dreams" with success in self-branding. The complete individual is broken down, deconstructed, demolecularized, and reconstructed in the image of the new Identity Establishment, comprising fashion designers, contractors, marketing experts, graphic artists, journalists, and a host of other related professions all bent on destroying and creating image identities to sell to the consuming public who are then urged to sell themselves. It is the new paradigm of animal husbandry and prostitution.

8.

THE INNER REVOLUTION

Fascism is not pacifism. It is a worldview that embraces struggle. It understands that Life is Strength and that we must not hesitate to engage in direct combat all those things that seek to bog down the human spirit in a mire of filth and materialism. Fascism has often been accused of being militaristic and war-mongering. We challenge the view as it is too simplistic and does not go far or deep enough. To call Fascism militant is to suggest that we have a chip on our shoulder. We do not. We have a large and legitimate grievance against the modes of life that have been created by materialists of every stamp. To call Fascism militaristic is to suggest that we play at being a fighting force. We do not play. We *fight*. Sometimes we win and sometimes we lose, but we *fight*. This treatment of our doctrine as mere militarism and war-mongering is shallow and superficial. The Fascist comes to Fascism because he craves tradition and a spiritual discipline that emphasizes the strengthening of his mentality and spirit.

The Fascist has found himself to be supremely at odds with the disorderly, vacuous, hollow forms of materialism and modernity. He seeks a better way; a deeper way. He seeks to follow a road that begins in himself, for it can have no other point of origin. To be sure, a Fascist begins with the struggle within himself. He knows a great and repellent, ravening beast lives within him, but that this beast is not a hopeless case. It can be tamed, trained, and taught. It is red hot steel that can be tempered and forged into a great and living weapon that will incinerate the darkness within and arise as a beacon for those who share his cause.

We affirm the immortality of the human spirit and its Source, the Supreme Being. However, similar movements of the past have been sectarian, and this has been a divisive force, depriving National Destiny of tools it might otherwise have brought together. Perhaps a new faith; a new religion, will evolve out of our work. It may or it may not. Whatever the case, we must stand together in affirming our faith in the immortality of the human spirit and the primacy of the Supreme Being. Fascism is religious in character but not sectarian. We support religion but prefer the ardor and disciplines of a religious life above religious membership.

Whatever our various faiths, what truly unites us is the Inner Revolution; our daily and continual struggle against materialism. We struggle against the values and agenda of those who would bind us to consumerist slavery; that is to say, against the laissez faire capitalists and international financiers. We struggle against the values and agenda of those who would bind us to their lies of planned economics and so-called social justice; that is to say, against the liberal Marxists and socialists. One wishes to bind us to slavery wherein we work doggedly at jobs that alienate us from ourselves in the hope that, one day, we may be able to afford products we do not need. The other wishes to bind us to a godless, pitiless state where we labor doggedly in order that we may earn the privilege of waiting in line for basic staples that are never there. One appeals to desires, the other to needs. Both are materialist. Both are corrupt. Both are in mortal danger so long as this movement has a breath in its body.

The human person was brought into being by the Supreme Being. It is not open for discussion in this movement. The human being has an immortal spirit endowed with intelligence and free will. In the Nation the individual can begin to realize the ancient, spiritual aspiration of enlightenment, which comes of embracing the greater group; the greater race. As a Nation, we are better able to fulfill our duty to our fellow creatures, we are better able to exercise our rights, and we are better able to express the powers of our transcendent nature.

The human entity, as an individual or as a Nation, is endowed with great power to enact the classical virtues; to do unimaginable good; and to carry out and delineate the highest standards of ethics and morality. The value of individuals, groups, or a Nation is not to be measured by standards of material wealth. That is a childish, base, primitive standard that cannot apply to a transcendent being. Social class is yet another false standard, for that is ultimately based on material power and we are back at the beginning. Ethnicity is also a material standard, referring as it does to characteristics of biology. Materialist standards are fine for unrestrained capitalists, communists, and savages. They will not do for real men.

We measure a man by his virtues, both civic and personal, and his achievements. We measure him by his virtues as they become known to us, primarily through the service he renders unto others. The work a man does for his fellow creatures, and the value he adds to the common stock of humanity, are the only reliable measures of human worth. What differentiates us from other movements is the faith we are willing to place in human individuals until they give us adequate reason to dismiss them. Until that moment, we place our faith in humanity's transcendent and immortal spirit, and more than that, we place faith in the Supreme Being. We place our faith in a Unified Nation. We place our faith in our National Destiny.

If you want something you have never had before, you must do something you have never done before. Therefore, before there can be a new State, there must be a new citizen; one that has not been before. This new citizen cannot exist until a new kind of person exists. A new kind must be preceded by a new individual. A new individual must be reborn from the inside out, and the inside must always precede the outside.

The First Revolution is an inner revolution. You have no right to try and change the world while you are lost in darkness and filth, and make no mistake: until inner revolution is achieved, you are lost in darkness and filth. Would you do any of your so-called good works if you were required to wear a mask and receive no credit for them? Would you engage in community service on the condition of total anonymity, even to those you are helping? That is the first proof. Until you are content to be invisible, you cannot become an idea and a force for good. All else is poisoned by the ego, and the ego, no matter what momentary benefits accompany its arrival, has but one goal: to glorify itself at the expense of all others. This goal is short-term or long-term but it is there and like the pirates of old, who changed flags when they got close enough to the ship they wanted to plunder, the ego's true colors will eventually be revealed.

The First Revolution is a revolution of spirit. The goal of this revolution is to overthrow materialism, which is enslavement to the values of the manifest, material world. Gain and loss, fame and infamy, wealth and want, desire and regret: all such things must be cast out. It is not sufficient to be moderate. A single drop of ink will pollute an entire glass of water, and so we must overthrow the inner tyrant and all his running dogs. Rearranging your inner and outer life so that you can have a life like you see in catalogs, magazines, and TV is nothing less than slavery. Until you overthrow the inner idols of the First Tyrant, you will not be free.

We hold it to be self-evident that Man is an aggregation of Spirit and Matter, and that the Spirit is Mankind's primary power. Unless we want the Fascist revolution to be an utter failure, every Fascist cadre must first stage within himself a revolution to overthrow materialism and egocentrism. Otherwise, any and all change we bring about in the world will be the continuation, under another name, of bourgeois domination, capitalism and socialism. Without an all-pervading spiritual revolution – a method of purification and improvement carried on by the individual over a lifetime – our cadres will not differ in any essential sense from the degenerates who have given rise to the horrors of the modern world, and who have acted upon a purely materialist conception of Life and History. It is the belief of Fascists that worldwide National Revolution can only be achieved by the creation of a New Man, a cadre who is not attracted to the trappings, titles, perks, and ill-gotten gains of power. Our New Man is interested solely in power itself. He knows power, in and of itself, is absolute and spiritual. He is interested in his power to shape himself and the world around him. He has no interest in stockpiles of worldly wealth because the world and all the wealth it contains is already his. The New Man is a living act of propaganda in the community in which he lives and works. It is equally the belief of the Third Position that the splendor of Western Civilization, viewed historically and culturally, has its roots in the doctrine and practice of Faith. If, therefore, the West is to regain its sense of Destiny and Mission, it must return sincerely and wholeheartedly to Faith. As each individual develops spiritually, Western Civilization will move forward to a New Imperium.

Since the degeneracy of the modern world is characterized by immorality and nihilism, it stands to reason that a regenerate world can only be built upon Moral Order and spiritual standards of living. It is vital that people understand that, in direct opposition to the nihilistic yammering of mass media, there do indeed exist such things as Right and Wrong, Truth and Falsehood, Good and Bad. It is moral dualism that distinguishes this world: a choice between Good and Evil, and not a rainbow of relativistic opinions and choices. Moral pluralism and moral relativism are lies. The basis of moral order is respect for the Truth. We hold many truths to be sacred to Moral Order, and one such truth is the primacy of the family. The Family is the cellular unit and center of any healthy society. If the family is strong, stable, and happy, that strength, stability, and happiness will belong to the Nation. For this reason, this Movement opposes any and all agencies and policies that seek to restrict, undermine or destroy Family Life. We oppose them with extreme prejudice. Healthy societies are made of intact families. The State must encourage the health and stability of the family. Parents must be the living example of purity and citizenship to their children as they teach them moral conduct, and oversee their education. If a parent does not structure their child's behavior, they must share in the guilt for all that child's wrongdoing. The State must be constructed in such a way as to help families provide a good education for children, and to encourage institutions that will assist the parent in training their child to be a contributive and spiritual citizen. We seek to raise people of superior strength and honor, not perpetual dependents. A perpetual dependent is a parasite.

Greed has poisoned the capitalist, lust has dominated the communist: the lust for power over people. Whether it is material profit or psychological thrills gained from dominating others, we have become demonic addicts.

Every technological advance serves only to further our sense of alienation from each other and the good earth. Every social change amounts only to further divisiveness, bloodshed and chaos. Knowledge that is not an outright fabrication serves only to insulate us further. Our supposed cleverness has led us to denounce God, the soul, and every noble impulse in the heart of man. Instead of feeding the masses, curing disease and ensuring better social conditions, we have used our incredible intelligence to increase poverty and want and to make the world more unsafe than it has ever been.

The Internet and the cellphone have become tools for unwarranted attack, exploitation, and the spreading of lies. These inventions were intended to bridge the gaps between us. Instead, they have acted as wedges, furthering the gaps and filling those gaps with a black and hateful bile. We cannot hate each other enough to satisfy the dark beast that raves within us. That beast claims men, women and children as victims and there is no depth to which it will not sink, from slander to child pornography. We have used technology to accentuate what is absolutely the worst in us.

To those who will listen, I offer this message: Do not give in to despair and darkness. The misery and sorrow in your heart can be used to unleash the dark beast in your heart, and nothing good can come from that. All this sorrow is the passing of the old world and the birth-pangs of the new. There will always be people who seek to enslave you and the entire human race in body, mind, or spirit. But the power they have taken from you will be returned to you, and so long as you have the fight in you, the great flame that burns in us can burn ever brighter and show us the way to the New World!

Do not allow them to exploit you. Do not wallow like hogs in filth, fit only for production and consumption! Light the candle in your heart! Burn away your darkness! Be what you want to be, not what the legions of the self-appointed say you are! You are free! You are not meant to be a slave for the capitalist; a test-case for the socialist! You are a free, dignified, and noble being, and it is high time you stood up and began to carry out your destiny, and your destiny is a great light: the light of National Destiny! This is yours! It is your birthright and your future and you must allow no one to take it from you!

Every religion that has existed has spoken of the essential divinity of man; his dignity and nobility, but when the total improvement of society became possible, those religions backed off on their word and gave the power that was yours to those who filled the coffers of the churches and temples. I am here to tell you: your essential dignity and nobility cannot be bought and sold, but they can sure as hell move mountains! So long as you buy the lie: the lie that you owe your obedience to a complex that does not safeguard your life and property nor uphold your family, you remain a slave. You must seize power daily! You must assert each day: I AM A HUMAN BEING! I AM THE REASON THE PLACES OF POWER EXIST! POWER LIVES IN ME AND NOT IN THE MACHINERY OF STATE AND INDUSTRY! You must make this the fact of your life and, living that fact, you must seize control of the machinery of State, of Corporation, of Church

and Community, and you must force it to serve the interests of the Nation;

not a body of professional politicians and their paparazzi lackeys! YOU,

COMRADES, ARE THE NATION! THE POWER OF NATIONAL

DESTINY IS YOURS! YOU HAVE ONLY TO RISE UP AND TAKE IT!

9.

THE FASCIST CODE

1. Fascism is Unity. Every Fascist is your Brother and your Comrade. All men are not equal, but we all share in the same struggle. It is your destiny to work and fight alongside your comrade and for that Great Cause to which you have both chosen to dedicate your lives. Always defend your Comrades and be prepared to aid them and their families.

2. The family is sacred as is our Cause. Spend time with your family and your Comrades. Never wrong, cheat, or defraud your Comrades. Never commit adultery with their spouse or significant other. Do no harm to children.

3. Respect your country; your Nation, and honor its traditions, symbols, and values.

4. Reject Materialism in all its forms. Capitalism, Communism, Hedonism, and Consumerism are all toxic and seek to incarcerate the Human Spirit.

5. Do not use drugs for pleasure, even if they are legal. Do not drink to drunkenness. Avoid using tobacco. Avoid pornography and prostitution. Keep your mind, your body, and your spirit free and clear of poisons.

6. Do not keep company with Liberals. If you must work alongside them at a job, maintain respect and professionalism, but do not befriend them. You can be sure that, eventually and in some way, they will try to corrupt you, for the Liberal cannot coexist with that which is pure.

7. Do not befriend the enemies of the Nation. Capitalists, Communists, Libertines and Liberals all seek to destroy you and what you have both inside and out.

8. Never sit idly by while your Nation is being slandered or abused. That is a passive form of Treason.

9. Maintain some form of daily spiritual practice, be it prayer, meditation, or study. Whatever it is you choose to do, keep it secret and private. Otherwise, you come across as a fraud and a fool.

10. Develop your strengths daily. Ours is a path of struggle, and only those who follow this path can achieve Power.

11. You must show respect for women, but you do not have to sympathize with all of them.

12. Keep your life simple, exercising moderation in all things and recognizing clearly what you do and do not need.

13. Gossip and slander undermine unity, and Fascism is Unity. Therefore, avoid gossip and slander at all times, especially concerning your Comrades in Fascism. Gossip and slander belong only in the mouths of paparazzi, Leftists, and women of low moral character.

14. Do not keep company with murderers, rapists, pedophiles, drug dealers, or terrorists.

15. Do not support increased bureaucracy, immigration, or social welfare. You will pay for them all and benefit from none.

16. You are not entitled to Liberty, Prosperity, or Power. You must become worthy of these things even if you have them. If you do not,

you will be stripped of them or you will never have them. You will

be an animal.

17. Work. Do not be a burden to your fellow taxpayers. In work is

dignity. All must work. Fascism is the Worker's State.

10.

CITIZENSHIP AND THE NATION

The practice of democracy has its roots in antiquity, when land-holders and those who had a legitimate stake in the affairs of the body politic were granted suffrage. The practice has undergone countless modifications since its first appearance in this world until the present, where it is equated with majority rule. Democracy grants citizenship to anyone who is physically capable of voting. The result is a mob of votes, not a Nation.

In granting universal suffrage, democracy castrates itself by equating the Nation with the majority, lowering it to the level of the lowest common denominator. As a result, even those with no stake in the Nation's prosperity, i.e. its professional victims, law-breakers, malcontents, and other assorted low-lives, are given a voice in the Nation's future. How does a rapist or home invader vote concerning matters of safety and privacy? How does a drug peddler vote on narcotics laws? How does a welfare scam artist vote when it comes time to decide how much cash will be poured into the welfare state? How does a murderer vote on the death penalty? Do you intend that such as these should have a voice in the future of the Nation? Are you *that* irresponsible? You would build a wooden galleon, fill its hold with gun powder, and allow a pyromaniac aboard? For shame!

The Nation must be considered from the point of view of quality rather than quantity. We do not ensure a brighter future for the Nation by granting suffrage to those who have a stake in its downfall, nor those who have no clear idea what the Nation is, nor those who wish to live off the labor and sweat of others when they themselves are perfectly capable of working. We do not secure the Nation's future by prostituting it to professional politicians. The Nation must find the expression of its political will in principles, not personalities. The People must be forged from a mob into a Nation by means of instilling pride in what they do in their various professions, by the enactment of laws that will not tolerate a breach of the peace or any harm to life, liberty, and property.

Of course, this begs the concept of Nationhood and Citizenship. Only a true and genuine citizen can be said to care for the overall health and welfare of the body politic. Only a citizen has a stake in the well-being of the Nation. It therefore becomes necessary to define a citizen not only in terms of his rights, but his responsibilities as well. It cannot be denied that liberty must go hand-in-hand with responsibility if the Nation is to steer its way out the present age of decadence and chaos.

Citizenship must include social responsibility. Social responsibility means individual sacrifice. The sacrifice of two years in the service of the Nation is a just and reasonable requirement for participation in the body politic. The State must find a place for those who serve, regardless of skill or aptitude. Not all service needs be military. Education, maintenance, clerical or administrative work can be an option for those not physically or mentally fit for military service.

Why service? Every right is conjoined to an equivalent responsibility. A two-year service requirement will ensure the rise of a citizenry whose vested interests in the well-being of the body politic are not merely economic. A citizen's interest in the future of the Nation must be expanded to include a sturdy political understanding and a healthy interest in social harmony. Service to the Nation ensures the rise of citizens who take the National life seriously. In short, it will give rise to citizens who are *Nationalists*.

Nationalism is patriotic, in that it grows out of love of the Nation. However, a Nationalist places the well-being of the Nation above globalism. The Nation is the primary concern of the Citizen, but this Nationalism does not and must not seek to supplant love of the Supreme Being and love of the family. The Nation is the primary concern of the Citizen as a political and economic being. As a person participating in elections, a citizen is responsible, loyal, and informed concerning the issues of the day rather than determined by party loyalties. He demonstrates this, in part, through his term of National Service. As a being of economic interests (among others), a Citizen has come to appreciate that the best and only real valid social program is work. He or she rejects social welfare for all except the truly invalid. All who are capable must work.

Citizenship must be the prerogative of those who have served the Nation. All others will have basic human rights, but they shall not participate in the body politic, for they have shown themselves to have no concern for its well-being and prosperity. Citizens serve the Nation.

The Nation is composed of citizens. Those who are not citizens are non-citizens. Citizens possess full rights under the constitution, whether such rights are held to be afforded them by birth or naturalization. Non-citizens do not possess these rights, but they may earn them under certain conditions, provided they have committed no crimes against the Nation or its people. The distinction is social and political.

The question of race has entered into public discourse concerning citizenship from time to time, and it is not absolutely assured that race has no role in the discussion. However, it is held that any member of any race can potentially and theoretically become one who has a positive stake in the preservation of the body politic and that Nation it embodies. In order for this to be true, one must understand and embrace the objectives and values of the greater Nation. The Nation must become his race, and while he may hold to his racial values at home, his life as a Citizen demands that he transcend the petty concerns and idiosyncracies of race.

It is purely absurd to suppose that Citizenship is conferred by means of paperwork and that this counterfeit citizenship entitles one to an immediate and full share of that socio-political and economic well-being that is the prerogative of those who have labored on behalf of the Nation and its people. The process of acquiring citizenship has been reduced to a process less complex than applying for a library card, and this *reductio ad absurdum* is a dire insult to the millions who have labored, served and sacrificed for the greater glory of the Nation.

True citizenship comes of embracing the Nation, its values and its goal as one's own. Each specimen has a responsibility to rise above the worst, most decadent qualities of its species, and seek to become something greater. One must strive to become more than white; more than black; more than Hispanic, Asian, or whatever. Individual biology must be subservient to the requirements of the Nation and one must be locked in a struggle to rise above all petty concerns. If that cannot be done, then one is not worthy of Citizenship and has no active role in National Destiny.

Provided one is not an alien to the Nation, one who has not yet earned the distinction of citizenship is held to be outside civilization as typified by the State. Before attaining the age of majority, such a person is its ward and, upon the age of majority, a subject. Certain basic rights are still assured. However, suffrage, the Right to Bear Arms, the privilege of holding public office, and the privilege of commanding those who serve the Nation must

be distinguished as the unique prerogatives of loyal cadres and Citizens.

Citizenship cannot and must not be a mere rubber stamp or sinecure as it

has become in recent times. It must be the exclusive right of those who

have demonstrated their worthiness by means of National Service. A

subject may be loyal and patriotic, but they are not vested in the body

politic to the same degree as one who has sacrificed to meet the needs of

the greater Nation.

This does not mean that one must reject one's blood and heritage. Pride is

not a crime, and there is no reason for anyone to be ashamed of their race's

higher aspects and accomplishments. However, each race has its trash

component. If this component cannot be eliminated, then it most definitely

must be contained and controlled, for there is a legitimate and an

illegitimate society. There is a part of every race that embodies the highest

aspects of the psychology, culture, and behavior of that race. There is another part that gives the rest cause for nothing but shame and disgust. It is neither feasible nor desirable to eliminate any one of the races. It is, however, feasible and desirable for each race to eliminate its worst aspects just as it is feasible and desirable for individuals to do so. The white racist points at the African, the Hispanic, the Asian or Jew and decries behaviors that can be found in any white neighborhood commonly associated with the term "white trash". Similarly, the African, Hispanic, Asian or Jew all point their fingers at other races, assiduously ignoring the faults that linger at home.

There have been a number of Fascist writers who hone in on race as the heart of all social problems and the touchstone of all possible solutions. There have been an equal number who dismiss it as irrelevant. There is a more reasonable and scientific way of approaching the matter. It is based on observation. Any member of any race can conspire to bring down the Nation. Any member of any race can play a vital and dignified role in National Destiny. It is a question of will, not chromosomes, and if we are unwilling to relinquish or grip on race and unwilling to focus instead on the difference between destructive and creative behaviors, then the destructive behaviors found in all races will continue as will the human tailspin toward extinction. If Fascism is opposed to materialism and since materialism is properly understood as encompassing an over-attachment to the physical, then it must be understood and accepted that race is physical and ultimately has no place in our considerations on National Destiny. It is for each ethnic, racial group to police itself or suffer degradation.

On the other hand, if we are not allowed to blame Muslims for the 9/11 attacks, then Whites of the present day are not eligible as vessels for the guilt of slavery. Turks are then not to be blamed for the Armenian genocide. Russians cannot be blamed for the atrocities committed over and over again in the Ukraine. The list goes on and on. It is a familiar biblical passage that can best be applied to the behavior of races: "Let he who is without sin cast the first stone." Members of all races have committed atrocities. Members of all races have been victims of atrocities. We do ourselves no service in rehashing history again and again. While it may be true that George Santayana said that those who forget the past are doomed to repeat it, this is not always the case. It is hoped that humanity has more mental sophistication than to believe in the rigidly applicable action of every axiom that comes down the pike merely because it sounds *awfully* catchy. The Jews were victims of persecution by the Nazis. Today, Palestinians are persecuted by Israelis. Not by all Israelis, but by Israelis nonetheless. It is well known that the Jewish community has not forgotten the Diaspora and the Nazi holocaust. However, not all Jews have learned the tolerance that other Jews preach. The same applies to Protestants and Catholics in Northern Ireland, Sunnis and Shi'ites everywhere, tribes in Africa, Polynesia, and indeed throughout the world. We are imperfect and we sometimes do terrible things. However, my comrades, there is no letting ourselves off the hook just because we feel ourselves to have been persecuted or marginalized.

If you wish to play a role in that noble work that is National Destiny, then you must see to your own behavior, and compiling endless catalogs of the atrocities and faux pas committed by other races has no place in this Magnum Opus. Any member of any race can act like an entitled, savage child. Any member of any race can achieve the Heroic Ideal and become a savior of their Nation. It is a question of Will and struggle and it begins inside yourself.

11.

POPULAR SUPPORT

We will transform society by creating the broadest possible base of support. The broadest possible base is the People. Without their support this movement dies. We must mainstream ourselves enough to enter public consciousness, while at the same time maintaining the integrity of our movement and our doctrines. We will succeed where Liberals and Capitalists will always fail because they cannot increase popular support for themselves without alienating the People.

It will be easier for us to gain popular support because the Liberals and Capitalists see the People as mere producers and consumers. To both, the People exist only to keep them in business. We will triumph because we aim to protect and serve the People. The People will look to us for protection because, historically, the failure of the systems of our enemies creates conditions favorable to criminal enterprise. Fascists are only too happy to fight against the criminal element.

We will begin to build our base of support by taking the cause of the outcast, the disenfranchised and the downtrodden as our own. Typically, they have nothing to give but their hearts and minds, and so they will steadfastly remember those who take up their struggle. To that end, Fascists ought to mobilize in their own communities. Go and help the poor, pick up trash from the streets, and inspire others. The aim is to come together with other Fascists and build a Fascist Volunteer Brigade for community service. Volunteer Brigades would utilize the intelligence, talents and skills of Fascist cadres. No one's muscle or brain is unsuitable. These Brigades would serve the interests of the community at large.

Volunteer Brigades will work on the social problems of the Community. This will put the Fascist agenda into true focus as we gather information, serve the People, and gain a clearer understanding of their concerns. The everyday concerns of the People must become our own or we have no prerogative as the guardians of National Destiny.

There must also be an economic push to our agenda. We must become integral to local economies; investing in local businesses, buying local products and, as we grow in strength, work toward the establishing of Fascist cooperative banks or, at least, financial programs through which we can help support the economy. This would partially be done through loans to local businesses, for one of the main enemies to our agenda is Finance Capitalism. We must not forget that, historically, the politics of the People almost always focus on land and bread.

We must become a visible force in the community and we must take up their problems as our own. And make no mistake, Comrades: their problems *are* our own.

12.

TRANSCENDENTAL NATIONALISM

Dualism assumes not merely a dual nature of things, but that there must be a fundamental and hostile dichotomy between entities. Traditional and modern society assumed to be antithetical to one another. However, this antithesis is more an imputation than an inherently existing distinction. The essence of the issue is a simple one: we have a physical and a metaphysical reality, and these two are intended by design to have an interactive and interdependent relationship. There is a duality to existence. Mankind has a mortal and an immortal nature. We are Being and Becoming; composed of visible and invisible components. The mistake made by many is to suppose that duality implies two theses cannot but be antagonistic toward one another. While they are certainly not the same and perhaps no desirable outcome can result of attempting to confuse the two, it remains that the harmonious operation of the two constitutes the whole action and essence of Human and National Destiny.

The spiritual and physical dimensions of humanity are not intended to be nemeses. That would be schizophrenic. The unitary or singular reality is meant to be dynamic, and this dynamism is only possible because of the existence of certain polarities that are contextual to it. These polarities are more or less definitive. Civilization progresses in the forward motion of innovation and this change takes place against a broad inertial matrix. The traditional society has been taken to occupy the position of inertia and the modern the progressive. However, to refine it further, it has been assumed that the inertial is always detriment and the progressive a

benefit. However, if we are to truly accept that categories can and do shift, then it is not only possible for the progressive to function as a detriment, but it often does so, particularly when embraced without a critical eye. It is not what is progressive that builds, but rather what is foundational or fundamental. Progressive is dangerously neutral, since technologies and diseases progress. It is not so much that progress is to be avoided, but rather that blind progression for progress' sake is growth out of control.

We assume that the redistribution of wealth would be the hallmark of progress toward a "just" society, but the proponents of this socialist trope are willing to gloss over the simple fact that their "redistribution" is rooted in theft. The wealth of x cannot be given to y unless it has first been taken from x. This may be done with legislative sanction, but this sanction does not by necessity reflect a rule of law. An opposing trope is universal responsibility, where all are liable to work and provide for themselves, but what they produce is theirs by right. This is usually assumed to be the theme of an exploitive bourgeoisie, grinding the laboring masses into paste. However, if every individual cell labors according to its true capabilities, the overall result will be a stronger, healthier organism. The individual works and moves against an inertial background that he believes is resisting him, but without which his movements will not even be possible. The individual works harder, producing more and experiencing greater satisfaction, when part of a corporative syndicalist structure where labor and management are no longer a hostile dichotomy but the two essential components of a working, but dual social and political entity.

And so we are confronted with the interchangeability and interaction of two polarities we have traditionally thought of as being intrinsically and with hostility opposed to each other. However, the reality is that polarity is dynamic, and that which is devoid of this dynamism dies. Civilization moves, as the cosmos moves, because of the tension between opposing powers or energies. However, it is not a given that all motion is of benefit. After all, an atomic chain reaction is very kinetic. A crowd the motion of which is devoid of a governing principle becomes a rioting mob. All force must have a governing principle or set of principles. Motion without limits becomes a detriment just as inertia without limits is death.

We must think critically when constructing our New Order. We must be certain that we are clear about what is indicated by such entities as the Nation and such categories as Nationalism. Again, the categories of motion and stillness permeate. National interests do not of necessity call for

unending conflict any more than an individual can be expected to struggle

within himself without relief for the duration of his existence. We must

bear in mind the ideal indicated by the story of the swordsman Matajuro.

Even the best troops must rest. And so our devotion to the Fatherland must

alternate between struggle and peace. It is by means of struggle that what

is harmful is overcome, and it is in peace that we have the time and space

to create. Otherwise, a Nationalist government could only be defined by

way of constant conflict. There we have the formula for dystopia and a

quick downfall.

We must proceed from the understanding that Nationalism is inseparable

from the idea of the Nation. Nationalism germinates as the practical

expression in a society's political structures, themselves the expression of

the sociocollective will. We must understand that the Nation as it is

employed in these considerations is a modern polity. Throughout the

ancient world, and throughout the Middle Ages, a Nation was

predominantly ethnic and cultural. The social and political dimensionality of Nationhood would very nearly have failed to materialize were it not for the upheavals of 1789, 1848, and 1914. However, we also must take into consideration the development of the New World and the unending struggle, the tension between plurality and homogeneity. Nationhood is born of dynamic tension and struggle, but it is solidified in unity and a movement away from this dynamism. A Nation must breathe in a rarefied atmosphere of struggle, even within itself, and it must also have a system of values already in place to ensure it will know when to exhale; when to allow things to stabilize. You do not get this through anarchy and nihilism. The one merely destroys. The other merely refuses to create once destruction has taken place. Peace and civilization do not come of those who believe in nothing and who want to destroy everything.

The rise of a Nation is a historical development. It is intimately bound to the narrative of its people, their values, and the growth of their strength. A narrow view tries to equate nationhood strictly with biology and race, and while these certainly will tend to play a role in the earliest stages of the growth of a nation, they do not of necessity constitute its entire life cycle. Ancient Rome was not merely a city; not merely a racial identity applied exclusively to those who farmed the land of and around the Seven Hills. From her earliest stages, Rome became a cultural and political entity, and this political entity was not defined solely in terms of the Roman polity, but was a cultural identity that was attractive to people beyond the confines of Rome. People of many different countries and ethnic backgrounds *aspired* to be Roman. Even during the time of the Republic there was an influx of what today would be termed emigration.

What distinguished ancient Rome's "nation building" from that of today? The Emperor Claudius may have been mad, but truth can come from anywhere. He said that Rome knew how to turn outsiders into allies. Let the PC crowd take note: Claudius did *not* say that Rome knew how to turn Romans into everybody else and everybody else into a shapeless, cultureless, unspeakable uncategorized mass of united flesh such as the

Liberals so desperately crave for whatever unspeakable purpose. Outsiders capable of military service were given land and made stakeholders in the Roman polis. In the event of war they would either fight to defend their land or be killed or sold into slavery. Merchants and tradesmen, crafts of every kind were also welcomed in Rome itself. However, they did not shape the Roman polity to suit them. They adapted because to be a Roman citizen was a privilege, not a right.

People came to Rome to better themselves. The ancient Romans were prejudiced just as many of us are prejudiced today. However, there was a general recognition that prejudice is not confined to one particular race. Anyone can experience it as receptor or producer. It is as natural to human experience as potholes are to roads both ancient and modern. One gets past it. So did the Romans. Foreigners who came to Rome adapted to Rome's culture. The Roman Senate did not meet to draft new legislation and re-create Rome every time a new foreigner emigrated to the city or the Empire. The foreigner adapted himself to the new home he craved. Or he left. It is always choice and will that decides these things, and to be unable

to assimilate or adapt does not indicate that the new place was too hostile.

It indicates that one failed to assimilate or adapt. Nationhood in ancient

Rome was culture, law, and a unified social identity. It was one face. Not a

wriggling mass of countless faces, each determined that the whole shall be

as him and demanding the entire organism adapt itself to him. That is a

disgusting and repellant chaos worthy of the most terrifying horror

movies. It is not Nationhood.

The Romans understood the Nation to be an identity and that identity

represented certain values and a certain way of life. The assertion of this

identity and its values was successful in terms of creating a united, if not

monolithic, society. To try to name the specific contents of Nationhood is

as ridiculous as asking a person to provide you with a list outlining who

they are. One does not explain identity. One lives it. This also applies to

Nationhood. It cannot easily or conveniently be explained or defined

except in terms of values, patterns, laws, and culture. These are taken as a unitary, metaphysical set. A picayune analysis as an attempt to render conscious the living reality is neither feasible nor desirable. We know the very word nation comes from the Latin "natio", which means "birth". This will help us to achieve a better understanding. The identity of who was Roman was, of course, not confined to birth. Roman citizenship was complex yet precisely adjudicated. However, nationhood as an extension of citizenship remains a simple, spiritualized, almost gnostic category. Romans grasped this transcendence. It can be known, but this knowing is distinguished from full cognizance. Ask a citizen to what the Nation is and their apprehension is more or less full. However, to point specifically to what actually and clearly defines it as what it is will elude even the most educated. Only the most devoted patriot, regardless of social standing or education, would easily, without hesitation or reservation, give you a fluent and forceful answer that makes its full intent plain. This answer may be discursive, but it may very well be the kind of answer that does not fit in the context of any conventional discourse. All know what the Nation is. Only the least eloquent could hope to truly express it.

13.

THE FAMILY AND THE SICK SOCIETY

The Family is built on love, trust, and respect. It is the nuclear unit of society, and society can no more exist without the Family than an organism can exist without its cells. It is that simple. The family must be clearly and rigidly defined against the vagaries of socialism, identity politics, and left-wing agendas and operatives that seek to subvert it. A family begins with a male and female parent. The parents conceive and give birth to one or more children. The true pattern does not and must not be allowed to stray beyond this traditional configuration, no matter how much federal funding is at stake. This definition is not rooted in rigidity or intolerance. It is rooted in Nature.

However, for little over a century there have been numerous attempts to usurp the family by groups, individuals, and movements who think they have something better. Social workers, human services organizations, charities, and the like all believe that, because they have uncovered a handful of unhealthy cells, that the very nature and structure of the whole organism must and shall be irrevocably altered to suit their continued endowment by the State. Social work, rooted in the erosion of the family, has been allowed to become a source of ongoing job-security rather than a means to remedying social ills.

The methods of remedying the dysfunctional family are insidious because sometimes they are necessary. However, those same demographics that would see the continuation of social service agencies also support legislations that encourage the development of those social ills that render families dysfunctional in the first place. Thus, the majority of people are unaware of the nefariously circular disease whereby they support the development of that which must ultimately destroy them. This carries over into the work of State functionaries. They weep when the State grows in power and celebrate when that same power trickles down to their wing of the government offices, unaware that both are eroding their credibility and their moral right to exist. The processes normally considered part and parcel of Justice do not even matter here. When someone alleges child abuse, the allegation does not have to be proven. The family is broken up and the child is put into foster care. Foster care is, in the majority, an abusive scam. More and more people become foster parents for the financial benefit they think they can accrue. Fewer become foster parents in order to do any true and legitimate parenting. In the meantime the abused child is often subjected to a level of abuse and neglect exceeding that which preceded it, but because this new arrangement has the sanction of a very corrupt Welfare State it is allowed to continue. The mandatory apparatus of State for securing the well-being of children and families assures a continuity of dysfunction.

Thus, our abused child is abused more and more, tossed here and there, and grows into an abusive individual who commits crimes. They are incarcerated and the State benefits further because its employees are thus guaranteed a paycheck and they will work harder to maintain their half of the apparatus of dysfunction. And so, decent, sane, rational, hardworking people are forced to subsidize the continued existence of, not a State, but a system that slowly and surely degenerates into a sicker and sicker automaton. I say automaton because the functions of the dysfunction apparatus are without discriminative consciousness and are self-perpetuating. The apparatus is also devoid of self awareness even though it is operated and maintained by human agents.

When an abused child devolves into an abusive adult and a criminal, perhaps a murderer, we place him in prison for the rest of his life at an enormous and fruitless expense to the taxpayer. Furthermore, prison-for-profit amounts to capitalism's most cherished dream: legalized slavery. We cannot justify using violent criminals for cheap labor as it has been shown time and time again that no system is immune from the exploitations of a mind that is kept in a cell with nothing to do but think 21 hours each day. Either way, we answer crime with crime and then the bleeding-heart liberals cry that the death penalty is just an eye for an eye and therefore barbaric. No, Bleeding-Heart. Your system is barbaric. It ensures that

society's sickness will continue because you have learned to profit by it.

Even when there is a death penalty, some murderers will sit on death row

for decades awaiting appeal after useless and expensive appeal, living at an

expense of millions of dollars per year. When states do make use of the

death penalty for violent criminals, they do so at the highest possible

expense with a 50/50 shot at efficacy. Death by lethal injection costs

hundreds of thousands of dollars. Even then, the procedure for the

execution costs hundreds of thousands of dollars and doesn't always work.

A box of bullets can be purchased for less than ten dollars, and the results

are guaranteed. Death by firing squad is quick, relatively clean, and

inexpensive. However, we allow murderers, rapists, pedophiles, drug

dealers, and terrorists to continue to live safely, well-fed and well-

protected at the expense of the innocent. This can and will be stopped. You

deter murderers by executing murderers, and not twenty years after the

fact, but within days or even hours of the establishment of their guilt. You stop the widespread epidemic of drugs by executing those who distribute

drugs. You discourage pedophilia by executing pedophiles. If the

citizenry knows that the penalties for heinous crimes and abuses are

unthinkable, they will not think of committing a heinous crime. It's that

simple.

A healthy society begins at home. Unless we uphold the sanctity of the

family and return to the legitimate sources of our social traditions

concerning the family, then we must be prepared to accept responsibility

for the continued entropy that hurls all manner of vileness and perversion

at our children and produces more and more heinous criminals. Then we

will try to staunch the bloodletting with a bandaid, all the while insisting

that the causes of these problems are somehow vital to a "free" society.

The "free" society pushed by our "free" spirits is a sick society. It is a

horrific gaggle of the walking dead.

14.

THE AMERICAN WORKER: DUPED AGAIN

As of 2017, nearly twenty-five percent of white men with high school educations are without work. Many of this same group are not only unemployed, but have stopped looking for work. It isn't because they are lazy. They aren't working because there are no jobs. They've stopped looking for work because they know it is a waste of time. Leftist media such as CNN have characterized this demographic as a "slice" of America. However, at 35 percent of the population, calling the Workers a "slice" of America is like calling the North Atlantic a droplet.

The liberals don't want to admit that their years of sorely misguided social experiments and social engineering and socialized this and that have led only to economic ruin. From his first days in office, William Jefferson Clinton broke his campaign promise to "focus like a laser" on the economy, and instead focused like a laser on gays in the military and the very corrupt and poisonous North Atlantic Fair Trade Agreement. As a result, Working Class Americans were once again thrown to the wind. The American Worker was treated no better during the Bush and Obama Misadministrations.

The last sixteen years have not changed much, either. The American Worker has been betrayed again and again. The most poignant aspect of this betrayal is that it was served up by those in whom the Workers placed their trust. In 2008, the United Auto Workers union signed an agreement with auto manufacturers which imposed unprecedented wage cuts on the company's 3,650 workers in Michigan and western New York. As a result, 2000 workers lost their jobs. Those who remained had their wages cut from $28 an hour to $18.50 and as low as $14.35 for so-called "factory support" jobs. New hires were brought in at $11.50 an hour with substandard benefits.

Of course, by the time UAW and NAFTA-related "reforms" were done, the

Detroit auto industry and that of western New York State were ravaged. The urban blight that these former manufacturing sectors have become is well documented. Jobs were shipped abroad, UAW pulled up tents and hauled ass out of town, and politicians shrugged and gave their usual "Who, me?" grin as American Workers were hung out to dry.

Detroit and western New York are not alone in their status as victims of Empty Promises. Take for example Scioto County in southern Ohio, where only 53.8% of men age 16 to 64 are employed. It should perhaps be mentioned that this was once the territory of former Presidential hopeless John Kasich, who spoke most eloquently of his prowess at creating jobs.

Scioto County has been ravaged by the GOP/Democrat gang rape of the American economy. Shoe factories that once employed thousands are gone. Steel mills that once provided work to thousands of families are boarded up and cold. Railroad yards that once saw hundreds of shipments of raw materials through their precincts are now shadows of their former selves thanks to the Obama Administration's hard-line "environmental" nonsense that, thanks to the Liberals, puts social programs before society. Lawmakers, greedy manufacturing executives, and union officers are collectively and directly responsible and culpable for each hungry family and each missing job. And yet, people line up to cheer and applaud the criminals responsible for this economic ruin just so they can say they once looked directly upon the insidious, false sunlight that is a politician, a rich man, or a union official.

Many workers don't have the education or training to make it in today's economy, and they have no means of getting one. Only 14.4% have a college degree, compared to 25.6% statewide and 29.3% nationally. 40 years ago, however, most workers didn't need to go to college to earn a decent wage.

However, even among the college educated we are seeing rising unemployment and poverty as lawmakers find it politically advantageous and lucrative for themselves to allow jobs to bleed out of the Nation.

There are some jobs available, but many of them pay minimum wage or just above. Local officials are trying to attract more employers, but the new positions often don't pay as much.

A typical working class man works a variety of temporary, poorly paid jobs. A working class male with a GED typically moves around, serving short stints at various jobs. Most of these positions are temporary, and the typical worker earns no more than $13.50 an hour for very repetitive, strenuous work with no advancement potential.

How long will the American Worker stand for this? How long before the Two Party Gang Rapists are called to task for their countless crimes against the American Economy, the American Worker, and the American way of life? How many factories must be closed down and boarded up? How many children must go to bed hungry tonight because some overpaid, useless lump of GOP or Democrat flesh and their Union cohorts, their

pockets stuffed from kickbacks, have allowed American jobs to be shipped

abroad?

Americans, isn't it time you woke up?

15.

CORPORATISM AND THE FASCIST ECONOMY

In the late 19th century the Proletariat in Europe began to take interest in the ideas of socialism and syndicalism. The pronounced emergence of the bourgeois class naturally conditioned the development of a new, urbanized, semi self-aware proletariat that sought optimal forms of organization for itself. However, much of the work done at that time tended to emphasize classism and class struggle. Despite the fury of socialist and communist rhetoric there was an impulse toward non-combative methods of reorganizing the political economy of the West. The intelligentsia, particularly those belonging to the Catholic Church, began to formulate an alternative to socialism which would emphasize social justice without the abolition of private property. The result was Corporatism. The term has been associated with popular notions about Big Business, but has nothing to do with this.

The corporation, when defined as a very large business, is not the same

entity as a corporation is it defined by syndicalism. The corporation as we

shall use the term is best defined as a major interest group having features

in common with both a syndicate and a guild. It is bonded by common

interests, not profits, and while there may be corporations of banking

professionals, manufacturing labor, and various tradesmen, these

corporations are not businesses per se. They are economic, social, and

political bodies uniting workers of common interest. The confusion merely

arises because the large business and the corporation as supported under

Fascism both make use of the same name, deriving it from the Latin *corpus*,

meaning "body".

A Nation's society and economy should be organized into major interest

groups, or *corporations*, and disputes can be more effectively negotiated

within this structure. A corporation is a unified industrial structure that

can become an effective partner to the machinery of State. Corporate

representatives settle any problems through negotiation and joint agreement, and act as a gauge for the higher levels of government by proposing regulatory legislation, from production costs to salary. Ultimately, corporative power is subject to override by the Head of State.

Corporatism arose in reaction to the egalitarianism and laissez faire capitalism that emerged after the French Revolution. In Germany and elsewhere there was a distinct aversion among rulers to allow markets to function without direction or control by the state. The general culture and heritage of Europe from the medieval era was opposed to purely individual self-interest and the free operation of markets. Markets and private property were acceptable only as long as social regulation took precedence over motivations such as greed.

Coupled with the anti-market sentiments of the medieval culture there was the notion that the rulers of the state had a vital role in promoting social justice. Thus corporatism was formulated as a system that emphasized the positive role of the state in guaranteeing social justice and suppressing the moral and social chaos of the population pursuing their own individual interests. Corporatism was flexible. It could tolerate private enterprise within limits and justify major projects of the state. Corporatism has sometimes been referred to as a Third Way or a mixed economy; a synthesis of capitalism and socialism. However, it is in fact a separate, distinctive political economic system.

Corporatism seeks to promote the natural solidarity of workers and entrepreneurs. This solidarity is natural in the sense of being proper and endemic to the social machinery of production. Remove either from the structure and production quite simply does not happen. Thus, the corporative spirit aims to create a smaller, more integrated industrial body. Managers quite simply must take on the role of leadership in every sense. Their work-related skills must be at their peak of development. Their conduct in the workplace as well as their conduct toward those who work for them must be impeccable. *Honor* <u>must</u> be the key word here. The enforcement of a list of mundane dos and don'ts in the workplace will not produce the necessary solidarity. Similarly, the workers must be as loyal followers. A fellowship must exist, protected by regulation emphasizing moral conduct and a strong sense of right and wrong.

Workers and management must rise above purely personal, material interests. The worker must learn to once again take pride in his work, even though modern technology has nearly done away with the concept of craftsmanship. He still must strive to do the best work he possibly can, for that work reflects upon him. Similarly, managers must strive to be leaders, and to raise the management of their company to an art form. The company must have the feel of a proud and noble family. This atmosphere is not impossible to create. It is a simple matter of ethics and proper economy.

We must strive toward rehabilitating the Worker. He must no longer be conceptualized as a faceless component of a faceless mass locked in a mindless routine to be rewarded with a pittance. The alienation of the

worker begins with this proletarization wherein he is converted from man
to machine part. This symptom is overcome by making the Worker a true
stakeholder in his company. Conditions must exist wherein the Worker
benefits when the Company benefits. We must also be rid of the parasitic
capitalist financier who has, at best, only a vague understanding of
production. The capitalist retains the lion's share of profits and yet his role
is almost entirely extraneous to Production apart from his ownership of the
capital. The financier has emerged from the entrepreneurial class to
become a separate interest from the entire industrial process. The resulting
orientation diverts profits and dividends away from the Worker and the
Company to maintain the financier's interest. I quote Baron Julius Evola:

> In a new corporative system, the capitalist, or the owner of the means of
> production, should instead assume the function of responsible leader, technical
> manager, and capable organizer of the businesses he owns, maintaining close
> personal ties with the most trusted and qualified elements of his companies, almost
> as if they were his headquarters, and being surrounded by loyal workers who are
> free from trade union control and are proud to belong to his company. (*Men Among
> the Ruins*).

It goes without saying that such a system will require more than the mere
giving-out of jobs. Evola uses the term "political consecration" to imply
that such a system's establishment would depend on a sacramental

mystique applied to industry and economy by the State. The role of

Production is sacred by virtue of its central role in maintaining the material

life force of society. The least we can do is to apply this sacramentalism to

that which keeps us alive.

What does this mean to our Citizenry? Citizens have a right to work for

their own self-interest. This self-interest includes the well-being of the body

politic, in which every true citizen has a stake, the community, and the

family. The citizen has a right to work and earn pay in order to support his

family without interference from greedy or incompetent management and

the corruption of trade unions, which have been shown to almost

universally possess ulterior motives. This corporate syndicalism seeks to

preserve the integrity of legitimate business. The shopkeeper, the

tradesman, the farmer, even the entrepreneur shall all be protected from

interference provided their enterprises do not violate social or ethical well-

being or present a threat to the Nation. Our policy must encourage

individual initiative. We would require only that entrepreneurs observe proper respect for the laws of fair wages and that they provide a safe work environment. These measures must not, however, make costs prohibitive or discourage economic growth. Workers, managers, and entrepreneurs shall all be encouraged to work together in a corporative body for the betterment of society and the Nation.

When business enterprises grow large enough to directly impact neighboring economies and economies at a distance; when the lives of thousands or millions will be impacted, it will be necessary that those businesses are syndicalized. This means that they shall be placed under the control of those who work in them. To paraphrase Marx, the Workers shall control production, their administration of business to replace that of shareholders who are not connected to the work. Workers in syndicalized business elect the leadership structure. Only current employees would be eligible for election or a vote. This leadership structure would become industry-wide as businesses vote on regional management for their corporative organization. Regional leadership would then appoint National representatives to a Corporate House.

Corporatism is not new. In fact, it has been a long time coming. It is the apex of a genealogy of ideas based in the philosophical concepts of Aristotle, Roman law, medieval social and legal structures, and even Catholic social philosophy. These share the basic premise that man's nature can only be fulfilled within a political community. The corporative worldview centers not on the individual but the political community. This community is highly developed so that all within its embrace may find the means of their own development as productive, independent, moral beings who nonetheless are integral, contributive units to the body politic and the community at large. It is within this context they find happiness and fulfillment.

16.

NATIONALISM

INTEGRALISM

POPULISM

Truth be told, we teach a more pure democracy than the traditional American concept. We seek to manifest the real and genuine will of the people, who when they are not irretrievably contaminated by liberal unorthodoxy seek to belong to something glorious and far greater than themselves because such is true human nature. The current system processes it surrogate "will of the people" through intermediaries such as professional politicians, media, and interest groups. Add to this an incompetent, bloated, self-serving electorate and you can be sure that the Will of the People has long been lost in the shuffle. The Will of the People is mitigated, even negated, to ensure that it will not become a danger to the bourgeois establishment. Indeed, it could truly be said that the Will of the People was never a factor in the machinations of this system.

The bourgeois establishment is composed of liberal socialists, wealthy republicans and their entourage. Right and Left are closer now than any moment in history to becoming meaningless distinctions. However, this is not the egalitarian utopia of the misty-eyed pot-smoker. It is instead, reminiscent of the last scene from George Orwell's allegorical novel Animal Farm, where the pigs and the farmers they had overthrown were indistinguishable one from the other. They are integrated, but this integration is not harmony. It is the botched splicing together of two inferior specimens to create a horrid, hybrid, disgusting political mutant that will do anything to hoard the general benefit for itself.

We advocate a system born out of struggle because Life is Strength. The Inner Revolution; the inner struggle, is the heart of Fascism. A man must struggle to overcome materialism within himself; overcome the urge to remain an infant suckling at the teat, and embrace a greater worldview. He must stop shirking the Heroic Ideal merely because it is "hard". He must stop crying about what he thinks is "fair". He must grow up. The Will of the People requires a strong leadership capable of focusing popular energies toward fulfillment of national priorities. This process, once in place, would completely bypass bourgeois considerations and liberal vagaries.

Our doctrine is despised by the Bourgeoisie, both liberal and conservative, Republican and Democrat. They hate it because our doctrine upholds that the Will of the People should be implemented without recourse to a moneyed political caste that seeks to further such excesses as unrestrained capitalism or the tyrannies of Soviet-style Marxism. They hate our doctrine because it reveals that true democracy is Nationalist, exalting the interests of the Nation even in opposition to globalist, multicultural demands.

Ours is a grass-roots movement at its heart. We do not seek approval from any source but the People. They are the sole authority from which this movement derives its power and mandate. The will of the people is clearly known in all things, and it is a Nationalist will. The People crave a strong movement and a strong Leader who is representative of who they are and who they hope to be. Such a leader will be well-versed in the Will of the People, not party politics and self-serving bureaucratic nonsense.

The People will hold themselves accountable for National Destiny. They will know the doctrine of the Party and maintain discipline within the Law. They will accept as an article of faith that each and every citizen is responsible for the well-being of the body politic. They will struggle daily to overcome materialism in themselves, their families, and in their communities. They will gain the ultimate triumph.

Because our Movement is seeking to uplift the Nation and exalt it toward its highest, best destiny, we are Nationalists. Because we derive our power to do this, not from a bourgeois power elite but from the People, and because we never lose sight of our common roots and daily priorities, we are Populists.

Our doctrine could therefore also be described as National Populism.

Although we uphold the ideals of authority and Imperium, we still

recognize that the People are the basis of all that we would create.

17.

A FASCIST IS ONE WHO SERVES

Anyone who goes about with the thought that Fascism seeks to fight the
legitimate powers of the military and police suffers from a basic
misunderstanding of what Fascism really is. Fascism seeks to create order
out of chaos. There can be no order; no public safety without law and
order, and yet we continually suffer with the spectacle of skinheads and
other violent types railing against the riot shields and breaking the
law. This betrays a basic misunderstanding, not only of Fascism, but of its
history.

In Italy, the great birthplace of Fascism, the *squadristi* did not arm against
the police. They did not try to destroy the legitimate powers of the State.
They did not seek to act as a menace to society. Having fought Italy's
external foes in the First World War, they turned and fought Italy's internal
enemies, and they recognized that the enemies of their Fatherland were the

Communists and foreigners who had no stake in the legitimately organized State. The squadristi were men of honor, many of them having served in the Great War. They understood Service to the Nation and National Destiny.

Fascism in America has not yet been so blessed. Today's "fascism" is a thousand splintered movements manned by broken toys broadcasting from basements, disaffected nutjobs, and sociopaths. Ironically, these are the very forces true Fascism seeks to remove from society. There are many self-styled "blackshirts" in America today who would think nothing of committing assault against the police or members of the armed forces. These are not the Legionnaires we need to give this Nation the rebirth it so desperately needs. These are nothing more than jail fodder.

Fascism must regain its moral decency and leave the punk-rock and the nihilism to those who have no future. We must be out in the community, not first broadcasting ourselves as Fascists and then demanding acceptance; but rather, we must be serving others. We should be helping

the elderly, protecting our communities, picking up trash from the

sidewalks. I do not mean beating junkies. I mean picking up trash. Go out

with a garbage bag and pick up the empty potato chip bags and beer cans.

Collect the dirty needles and dispose of them properly. Bring coffee and

donuts to the Police. Raise money for the veterans in your community.

Show the People of your community that you are a man of trust and honor.

Integrate yourself. After all, integrity is our core value!

This community service must come first, before we presume to be National

Heroes. If we are not willing to take up a broom and do the very dirty,

unglamorous, undramatic jobs that need doing in and around us, we have

no right to expect the People to entrust us with defense of their virtue and

interests. It is high time that Fascists stopped whining about their

machismo and started using it. Be a man. Go and do a dirty job that no one

in your community wants to do; something that doesn't involve being violent. A legionnaire serves his People. He doesn't frighten them. He

serves them. A Fascist is "one who serves." He is *samurai*.

18.

TEACHING THE YOUNG

We are losing the fight for the soul of youth. The demythologized civilization of the last 300 years has not provided young people with the forms vital to the unfolding of the maturing human spirit. The atheist and the agnostic may decry religion and forms of mystical activity all they like. It will not change the fact that the human psyche has a very real need for these forms. They are the intangible trellis upon which the developing soul grows, much in the same way ivy will do. These forms have been instrumental in assimilating the youth to his society and they point the way for his future development as an actualized and living embodiment of the heroic ideal. One glance at the headlines of today should reveal the problem. Pregnant 12-year-olds, children of younger ages committing murder, using and distributing drugs, being forced into lives of organized criminal activity, and dead before they are 40: Our children are being forced to live in a cycle that is little different from that endured by Dark Age serfs, who were also dead by age 40. The horrors endured by our young people are reflective of the dreadful lack of proper values, the impurity, narcissism, and sense of unjustified entitlement persevered in by their parents. We may despise young people for their behavior, but nearly all behavior is *learned*. What are they learning?

Perhaps it would be more instructive to delineate what they are *not* learning. They have no respect for their own civilization or their elders. Respect has been replaced with the idolatrous vices of consumerism and political correctness. It is being replaced with entitlement, irreverence, and an ever growing sense of deracination. Between media, consumer culture, and a generation of parents too materialistic to care and too weak to discipline them, our youth have degenerated into lost souls at best and, at worst, savages.

The young must be taught filial piety, loyalty, and service. While in the more impressionable stages of their early lives, they must learn filial piety from a good, stable, traditional family. They must be taught respect for their elders and respect for the rules of the house. They must learn what it means to be a citizen of the Nation, and to render due respect and loyalty to the Nation. They must be taught service to others. It will undoubtedly be the more challenging of the three, but to convey to the young a sense of unselfishness will go furthest toward producing strong, loyal, critically thinking subjects of the Fascist State.

The young must be taught prudence and trust by the prudent and the trustworthy. They will learn and replicate behaviors they see in people they admire. If the role models in their lives are drunken, obnoxious, foul-mouthed, entitled reprobates, there is a better than average chance they will follow suit. Most of our efforts at reconstructing damaged youth through various social programs have only served to exacerbate the problem. The youth of today, steeped in the consumer culture that encourages them to act on impulse, must learn self-discipline and or they will destroy their lives.

The young must be taught kindness and benevolence by the kind and the benevolent. These are rare types. We live in an age when people proclaim themselves childcare specialists by the horde, and then the nightly news becomes a parade of abused children discovered in the dysfunctional precincts of a daycare establishment that should never have been licensed. In schools, everyone competes to be the biggest hero, the biggest sycophant to children. However, our children are learning spite, backstabbing and manipulation more than kindness and benevolence. These lessons are not learned in a vacuum.

The young must learn the arts and sciences and they must study the classics. They must be taught by teachers, not bureaucrats and activists. Education has degenerated into a freak show of standardized tests, politically correct propaganda, administrative nonsense, participation trophies, hypersensitivity, and unionism. Only the imparting of knowledge and the inculcation of character can be referred to as education.

The young must be taught respect for the Law by their parents, Law Enforcement, and the Community at large. To respect the Law is to respect the life and property of others. However, the ethos of the present age offers the option to view respect for the lives and property of others as optional rather than mandatory. This vital requirement of civilized society is neglected and abused everywhere. To reinstate it will be an uphill and vitally necessary fight.

Fail to teach the young properly and you cripple them. Fail to teach the young properly and you cripple the future. All the evil they do shall fall to your account as well as theirs. Teach the young properly and you share in the good they do, even should they forget you. You do this for the future, for you too were once someone's future. All have a part in civilization and its continuity, and this continuity begins with respect.

The young can only learn proper behavior from proper role models. It is that simple. In an age where the goal of many parents is to be their children's "buddy", there is no dignity in the role model. Hence, what is termed a role model is really no more than another peer. The child is not expected to demonstrate deference and respect to a peer. The peer is viewed as an equal, and there should be no mistaking that a parent is not the equal of their child. The human reality is inherently hierarchical. It just is. We do not owe fairy-tale explanations about equality or apologetics for the legitimate exercise of parental authority. The Family is integral to the Fascist Order, and we will never be apologetic about this. Remember that one of the Left's highest priorities is the erosion of the family and its eventual destruction. 100 years of subversion have not altered this priority. We must therefore become equally insistent on upholding the primacy of the Family in society.

19.

THE HEROIC IDEAL

A hero is a person who possesses those qualities that are necessary for his culture to thrive beyond the level of mere survival. The hero has his universal aspect inasmuch as every culture has its heroes. The specific traits of the hero are specific to his culture. Heroism has been the target of repeated attempts to disprivilege, marginalize, or otherwise disengage it from Western culture at large. It shall be my goal in this chapter not merely to acquaint the reader with a concept of which I am sure most are already aware, but instead to make the reader plainly aware that referring to this impulse as the heroic *ideal* in no way places it beyond the reach of human capability. It is as vital to you as your heartbeat and your breath. Modernity has stripped civilization of the heroic ideal, with the result of the general decline of the West.

The milieu of the hero is struggle. It is the primary means by which heroism is made manifest, and the mythologies of the world would be as flat and empty as bicycle tires if struggle were removed or sanitized out of them. On a social scale, struggle manifests as war, in which combatants and civilians stand to lose everything. It is a gigantic gamble. However, it also generates a matrix wherein people may detach themselves from everything that is theirs by association or attachment. In this space, individuals have a rare opportunity to discover who they unequivocally are. It is this moment of gleaming self-knowledge that is vital to the heroic ideal and to the life of every culture, no matter how bland and weak the forces of subversion and political correctness try to render it.

The Hero is humanity's response to the randomness, cruelty, tragedy, and destruction of life. He rises from the relative obscurity of the common masses to emulate the very best qualities of his society. It is through this emulation that the Hero gains the prerogative to separate from the herd, delve into the darkest recesses of that which threatens his society, gain the utmost sanctuary of danger and reward, seize the essential treasure that will salve his people and Nation, and return triumphant. Because of his labors, not termed Herculean by accident, the Hero is the savior of his people. Even should the primordial dangers of the supernatural dark overwhelm him in the end as they did Siegfried, the Hero becomes the primary type of his civilization; the vessel for all the qualities his society reveres and the key to its revival.

This ideal of heroism and differentiation is nothing less than a spiritual, supernatural dimension. The heroic ideal, in other terms, is nothing less than a sacred path beyond ideology or theology, and beyond even my writing about it. The heroism of struggle is a path of transcendence from the regular, everyday self to the greater selves of group and the race, to the ultimate or higher self, characterized as the Supreme Being. Make no mistake: this path is not for the faint of heart. It is not the ersatz, rummage sale spirituality of the New Agers and their curio shops and ineffectual books and useless imaginings about how thinking about moonbeams and reeking of patchouli will make you magical. This is a path of suffering and pain and, very often, alienation. One who chooses to walk this path will be, for a time, alone and without help. Sealed into the tunnel beneath the mountain, so to speak, one who seeks the heroic ideal may find himself with no more aid than a torchlight. He will be unsure of the path. However, he must walk the path. Eventually, he will arrive at the light and the company of Heroes.

Heroism is a timely virtue, particularly in this age of advanced moral decay, out-of-control materialism, narcissism, and atheism. Since the middle of the 20th century, Western democracies have advanced from moral relativism and the interrogation of moral values, to a casting off of morality altogether in favor of a highly narcissistic brand of consumer-based hedonism. Sexuality, ever the modern obsession, has become more and more acute in its appetites as spiritual seeking is dropped off more and more by people who were deluded enough to equate spiritual living with a constant parade of miracles affirming the primacy of their own selfhood.

The soft religions emerging in the 20th century, from Wicca to Thelema, have all promised to put human beings on a decadent, hedonistic peak that they very mistakenly equate with godhead. Misinterpretations of Hinduism, Taoism, and Buddhism have comforted Westerners in the cocoon of subtle egoism rather than expose them to the harsh, cold, unforgiving light of the reality we all have had a hand in constructing. If this is an age of darkness, then we are the ones who turned the lights off.

The hero departs from the easy, predigested, prepackaged world of his herd with all its instant gratifications, gadgetry, and nonsense into the Great Wasteland. The myths of mankind affirm this with thousands of images all delineating the same basic story. In that wasteland he is purged of all his infantile wants, needs, and thoughts. The process is not pleasant. "Pleasant" is for the world left behind. Heroism seeks supernatural might and wisdom. It is a path every sincere, recovering addict has walked. Every mama's boy who, through hardship, has weaned himself from his overbearing, enabling family has done so. Every loner who has recognized the treacheries and inadequacies of the herd for what they are, every

humanity-loving misanthrope, everyone who knows that salvation begins

with crucifixion; walks this path even if they are largely unaware of it.

The problem confronting Western societies in this materialistic and

demythologized age is the absence of forms, social and religious, that can

assist the individual in actualizing the heroic forces within. Traditionally,

this was the work achieved by rites of initiation and passage, wherein the

young were, after being brutally and symbolically removed from the

protective womb of childhood, were made fit psychospiritual vessels for

the power to help carry their civilization forward. The ancient world of the

Mediterranean had the various Mystery Cults. From the sacred grove at

Eleusis to the mysterious shrine of Delphi, our ancestors sought to

integrate the heroic ideal and its associated mythology into their lives. The

Northmen, the Maori of New Zealand, the natives of Papua New Guinea,

and the various Amerindian nations; all of these and many other cultures

have constructed rituals for the intimate emulation of heroism in their lives. Modern Western civilization, however, having ravaged its primordial value systems and traditions during the so-called "Age of Enlightenment" has given itself the deluded message that it must, to assuage itself of some imagined burden of guilt, render itself as materialistic and atheistic as possible. It is rather like a general who, confronted by an opposing army, orders his men to smelt their weapons and contract a wasting disease.

In this waking world, Heroism is the accomplishing of one's moral duty. It is not the sports hero or the celebrity who wants all the cameras pointed at themselves. It is the parent who sacrifices everything for their children. It is the police officer who walks into a dangerous hostage situation knowing full well he may get shot and killed. It is the fireman who rushes into a collapsing skyscraper because he knows where he can find that one last person to be saved. It is the brave Fascist who stands tall in the face of all the foul opposition the Left can muster, fully aware that he may get a rock in the face but, for the sake of all he loves and believes in, is willing to make his enemies remember him well into their old age. It is the addict who puts the needle or the bottle down, knowing he will not get another fix or another drink and the next several days of his life are going to be pure hell. Adherence to duty is a path by which the hero triumphs over his fears, passions, and downfalls–all those Achilles Heels that bind him to the vagaries of material illusion. Duty is our connection to the Supreme Being. This is not church devotion or that "divine love" that has not manifested in any of the world's great religions in millennia. It is a way to tap into a superhuman source of power and wisdom. It is the path from man to Superman.

We all face an internal and outer war. Far from suggesting that one is greater than another, I would emphasize that both are of equal importance. The internal struggle is against materialism, narcissism, and the atheistic/agnostic impulse that extends from narcissism. The external war is against a culture and civilization that utilizes materialism in the ways I have discussed in previous chapters as a means of subversion and pacification. Although both struggles are equal in importance, the interior struggle is the more arduous. Once it is accomplished the outer struggle will develop into victory as a matter of course.

The outer struggle of the present time is largely manifest in programs of ideological warfare. The heroic type, largely demonized by the materialistic left because of the support it naturally lends to movements and forms traditionally considered "far" or "ultra" right, is the primary *persona non gratis* for nearly every liberal program and construct. It is nearly Public Enemy Number One. This is to be expected in a civilization that has been largely hijacked by those forces actively seeking its downfall.

How, then, shall the individual know heroism in himself? There will be a pervasive sense of expectancy beyond the body and its environs; a sense of gathered force without a particular object to which it will direct itself. There is a sense of a momentous threshold approaching, the precise parameters of which are more or less a mystery. This is greater than the petty dramas and action of the silver screen, and because it is so foreign to most of us, it may seem completely at odds with all our expectations. The infinite is beyond our human sensory makeup and so we may only sense it faintly. However, once the heroic ideal becomes operative in us, we cannot help but intimate its presence. The only choice after that is to jump into the fray and make the Hero manifest, with no thought about who or what we shall be or what shall be the result. Ours is a doctrine of action as much as thought. Ours is a path of Triumph.

What is proper to a warrior's ethos and the heroic ideal is that one learns to devote oneself with a total devotion. There can be no such thing as being a little committed to the path. There can be no such thing as a slight devotion. Every activity of one's life must be done with as much care, assurance and dignity as if that act were the most important activity in the entire cosmos. Naturally, this must extend to one's political and social life. The general public, inclusive of our foes, must come to understand that, should they engage us, they will have one hundred percent of our attention and commitment. We must have no happy enemies and no unhappy friends. With enough devotion, one ceases even to care about personal survival. It is at this point that one has begun to overcome the gross demands of flesh, bone, and ego and has embraced the tip of the divine outcropping in us. We grasp the enormity of our true heritage. We begin to achieve oneness with the greater selves; those of our group, our race, our Nation and, in time, the unspeakably powerful Divinity that shapes our destiny. This is not, however, the pseudo-intellectual titillation of New Agers and armchair mystics. Instead, it is altogether new life that truly dispels weakness, ignorance, and all forms of spiritual darkness. It is power and fury. It is a storm of serenity. It is a transhuman exuberance with which one marches into the gaping maw of that which would engulf and overwhelm us and destroys that repellent beast from within. We emerge from this seeming death triumphant, our lives, our existence, our very spirit reborn.

Complete self-transformation is inherently combative, for the lower self

resists change due to the inertia inherent in part of human nature. Modern

man is a creature of stasis and comfort. The materialist paradigm has

sufficiently demythologized our worldview and psyche that to reach the

ideal will require considerable effort. It requires tremendous self-discipline

to undo the materialism, inauthenticity, and pathos of the modern psyche.

However, there will be an inevitable breakthrough. For a tremendous and

world-transcendent power burns fiercely within man, though he has spent

the better part of the last 400 years attempting to bury, deny, or sanitize it

out of existence. Revealing man's heroic essence and reintroducing him to

the mythic dimension of his existence is tantamount to the application of

dynamite to an underlying stratum of bedrock in order to retrieve the

treasures of the Earth.

The warrior lives beyond doubt and fear. His conduct is always direct and

calm. Just as warriors in ancient society came to take pleasure in the

dangers and trials of their profession, we are called upon to extract the

Earth's treasures; to find truth and meaning in our suffering and to know hardships as nothing less than opportunities for our true Nobility to show forth. Furthermore, the heroic ideal grows out of the hierarchical arrangement of society and man's inherent urge toward organizing himself into hierarchies. The heroic ideal is not egalitarian, for the warrior will only accept those he can respect as brothers-in-arms. His relationships are well-defined and based on the virtue of loyalty.

Many Westerners conceive of the hero as a passionate type. They think of Lancelot seducing Guinevere or Bruce Li shrieking wildly as he inflicts his fighting skill on the villain. Such betrays a general misunderstanding of warriorship. Go and meet with a United States Army Ranger; a Royal Marine; a French Legionnaire. You will find no one more dispassionate and still deeply committed to the hero path. This ideal can even be found among the most effective police officers and fire fighters. It is rooted in detachment. The hero path is duty and commitment, not passionate intensity. He is like a mountain of rock in a storm. He cannot be moved.

His is full of certainty and calm when confronting what must be done. One divests and simplifies.

A traditional story of the Japanese samurai serves to illustrate the open simplicity of the heroic ideal. Matajuro Yagyu, the son of a famous swordsman, was a source of shame to his father due to his mediocre skills with the blade. In order to remedy the situation, Matajuro went in search of a master who could improve him and his skills. In time, he found the famous swordsman Banzo. Banzo was a highly discriminating teacher. "You wish to learn swordsmanship from me?" asked Banzo. "Forget about it."

"But I am willing to work very hard to become a master swordsman," persisted the youth. "If I work very, very hard, how long will it take?"

"The rest of your life," replied Banzo.

"I cannot wait that long," explained Matajuro. "I am willing to do whatever you require of me if only you will teach me. If I become your slave and work like a dog, how long before I become a master swordsman?"

"Ten years," Banzo relented.

"But my father is getting old, and soon I will have to take care of him," said Matajuro. "If I work myself half to death, how long would it take me?"

"Thirty years," said Banzo.

"What are you trying to do?" asked Matajuro. "First you say ten years , then thirty years! Give me a straight answer! I will do anything to master this art as soon as possible!"

"In which case," said Banzo, "you will have to devote no less than seventy years to mastering this art. A man as impatient as you cannot learn quickly."

"Very well, Sensei" the youth relented, seeing the master's intent, "I agree."

Matajuro was forbidden to speak of swordsmanship and forbidden to touch a sword. He cooked for Banzo, cleaned his house, cleaned the yard, cared for the garden, and cooked the meals. There was not a word spoken about the art of swordsmanship. After several years, Matajuro was still working for Banzo. He began to despair, thinking he word never learn the art to which he had devoted his life.

One day Banzo crept up behind him and without warning gave him a sharp strike to the back of his head with a length of bamboo. Matajuro resolved to keep a better watch of what was going on behind him.

The next day, when Matajuro was preparing the midday meal, Banzo attacked him with a frontal assault he was not prepared for due to watching his back.

A few days later, as Matajuro was raking leaves in the yard and keeping vigilance to his back and front, Banzo swiftly and suddenly attacked him from the left. The master disappeared as quickly as he had appeared. Bewlidered, Matajuro resolved that now he must watch his back, his front, and his left side. Within the week, Banzo began attacking from the right side as well.

Throughout the day and sometimes at night, Matajuro found himself having to defend himself from sudden, unexpected attacks by the Master. At any moment every day there could be a fierce and unexpected blow from any quarter.

In very little time, Matajuro made his master proud. Under Banzo's

unorthodox tutelage, Matajuro became the greatest swordsman in Japan

Embracing the heroic ideal, Fascism offers us life as a warrior in a spiritual

army. This differs vastly from the standard liberal view of the military as a

necessary evil that should only be taken out of the box in time of war and

then immediately hidden away from "polite" or PC society as soon as the

threat is contained. True civilization is heroic and virile. True manhood is

achieved in the spirit, in developing the warrior's outlook on life.

In this age of shameless materialism, everything is thought to be a matter

of quantity. Men are judged, by each other as much as society at large, by

the amount of money they have, the number of times they can lift heavy

objects, by the amount of money they spend on their cars, and the list goes

on. The PC-masters have striven to create a society without conflict; a

"nice" and "tolerant" society. Men have been marginalized en masse as feminists, ever unhappy and unsatisfied, have pushed women to invade facets of life that were intended to be exclusively male. The result is wholesale degradation and a slovenly society. We must reclaim our virility, our power. This begins when we achieve scorn for what is "easy" and "nice". Basically, while we must be humane, we must stand up and defiantly proclaim *that only men shall define manhood*. We shall reclaim the heroic ideal by manifesting the Hero that lives in us, against all distaste, liberal ideology, and opposition. We are the pioneers of the coming Age of Heroes.

20.

FASCISM AND ANTIFASCISM:

ORDER VS. CHAOS

Fascism embraces dictatorship because dictatorship is perennial. It

represents one of the eternal verities existing outside man and the world;

that of order out of chaos, which can only come about by means of control.

Any force left undirected is wasted in terms of its connecting to the

primary object or it is perverted into something accomplishing the aims of

its opposite. When populace, State, and structure are without an

overriding, governing force, these will slowly and surely decay into party

politics, mob rule, and social disorder. This process is not new. The

Romans suspended the freedoms of the republic when Italy was in danger.

The National Convention did the same thing in France. Fascism establishes

a permanent dictatorship, or a dictatorship as part of its apparatus, because

Fascism recognizes the constant threat posed by those forces, ideological and physical, that tend toward decay and social disorder. The only solution is strength of leadership, not a popularity contest where all is reduced to the lowest common denominator.

Disorder and Chaos are perennial, but their proponents fail to recognize their own contingent nature. They are not needed for humanity's forward movement, and make no mistake: Humanity exists to make progress; to develop spiritually as well as physically. However, this progress always has its opponents. In these times we have the Antifa ("Antifascist") movement. It consists of masked thugs inciting riots, beatings, vandalism, and other forms of mass disorder in opposition to what it believes to be Fascism. However, all Antifa attacks on Fascism are not attacks on Fascism. Indeed, the rank and file of Antifa, as well as its supposed leadership know nothing of Fascism at all. To begin with, there is currently no Fascist government anywhere in the world today. There are authoritarian governments, but these are not Fascist. The two are different even if members of Antifa are too mentally lazy to comprehend the difference, and they are. Antifa's "attacks on Fascism" are nothing more than violent exercises in mob-based oppression of those who to any degree present opposition to the agenda held by the various Antifa infestations. Although Antifa characterizes itself as a mass movement (because a movement is less organized than a party), it is actually a gang or an organized mob. In many cases, it is nothing more than a crowd gone out of control with one or more voices directing it toward certain ends.

Let there be no mistaking this: Antifa operatives are cowardly hypocrites. They decry the faceless character of regimes while donning masks. They hide behind these masks while committing violent crimes and destroying property and assaulting the legitimate forces of the Law and the Police. The last thing most Antifa operatives wish to do is to have their true identities known and tied to their crimes. This is not done in some "revolutionary spirit", but rather because they haven't the courage to accept the consequences of their actions. Antifa has no true ideology other than attacking people and property they believe to be associated with principles or institutions not meeting with their approval. Indeed, Antifa operatives are little more than childish, moon-eyed malcontents. They are not even idealistic. Quite the opposite, their agenda is materialistic. It seeks to aggravate class tensions, promote Marxian collectivization (to be imposed on everyone but Antifa), and to create a dystopia ruled by the State as the Eternal Mother. Strictly materialistic, Antifa denies Tradition; that broad category of eternal truths. They reject anything greater than themselves, even their own movement should it demand sacrifices they are neither strong enough nor mature enough to make, such as working or not abusing narcotics as a lifestyle. They are narcissistic materialists. They even reject notions of gender based on their delusional misunderstanding of equality of the sexes. They also embrace this imaginary gender equality/neutrality because, truth be told, they crave universal promiscuity. Put simply, Antifa operatives wish to couple with everyone and everything, perverting the human race into a shapeless mass of sexless flesh. To the orthodox or traditional religious observer, this combination of hedonistic promiscuity, narcissism, materialism, and desire to create chaos is enough to equate Antifa and its Liberal champions with the devil's own spawn. They must be stopped. Their success will be the Nation's funeral wreath.

Fascism is the only legitimate opposition to the Antifa movement and their anarchic disease, itself one of the many horrible outgrowths of Liberalism. Whereas our enemies crave to divide the Nation, Fascism emphasizes unity. We embrace political unity because it is only by virtue of a singular ideology that society can be preserved against anarchy. Furthermore, anyone with even a glimmer of intellect knows that the disjointed system currently in place, with all its partisan politics and divisive rhetoric can only benefit party leadership and those who benefit by maintaining party infrastructure. Partisan politics benefits bureaucrats, not the People. We embrace philosophical unity because a Nation governed by multiple value systems and ideologies will disintegrate. We strive for social unity, by which we mean all classes and races in cooperation with one another, not forced to live and breed together. Everyone has a role to play in National

Destiny, but there can be no "protected classes" without there also being persecuted classes. To use one's intrinsic status as a bargaining tool is immoral. Fascism embraces all as potential Citizens of the Nation while not forgetting that hierarchy and inequality are hard wired into human nature. We also strive for economic unity, for there is nothing more dangerous to human society than classism and class struggle. All classes are vital to our National Destiny. That is why Fascism seeks to create corporative syndicalism. I will deal with this in far greater detail in a later chapter.

The creation and enforcing of this unity is an authoritarian project, for unlike its opponents, Fascism does not disguise its authoritarian character. This authoritarian conduct of the Nation is accepted in times of crisis, but must become our baseline stability because Fascism is an affirmative answer to the question of social entropy. No one cares to think of it, but entropy is more or less constant in an impermanent world, and this entropy, as we have seen throughout history, creates monstrosities of

Liberalism and libertinism. No one in the so-called Democracies of the world cares to admit that the other polarity of Liberty is Duty. They feel the need to prevent a stabilized society because the wooly so-called holistic thinking of the last several decades has them swallowing wholesale the notion that stability is stagnation. Nothing could be further from the truth. The chaos that engulfed Spain 80 years ago was instability. The Bolshevik Revolution was instability (and 70 years of enforced instability). Watts, Division Street, Stonewall, Ferguson, Baltimore, etc. are all prime examples of the instability beneath the surface leading to erupting chaos. However, the underlying cause of these riots was not injustice. It was the failure of the State to ensure the unity and stability of the Nation as a total phenomenon. Make no mistake: the current conditions of political life put all of us in a constant state of danger and the measures necessary to insure true independence, stability, unity, and salvation must be taken now or we will all face an unspeakable catastrophe that will make the L.A. Riots of 1992 look like a playground tiff.

Fascism and its forebears arise in response to societies in crisis. It does not have a single character, but is adaptive and formulates according to the unique features and problems of the country giving rise to it. It is the response of a nation's autoimmune system, and its failure to arise in societies in crisis signals the failure of those human structures that are intended to preserve the life of that society. A body that does not respond to invasion by foreign bodies is close enough to gangrene and death that some would say it may be best merely to allow the disease to run its course and make the funeral arrangements. The inspiration and reactions of Fascism to the crisis will tend to be based on the clearest notions of the Nation's heroic past held by the men of that Nation. Let there be no mistaking that Fascism is a reaction and a restructuring of society based in Tradition in the transcendental sense. However, Fascism is fundamentally nationalist and so certain aspects of a given country's Fascism will not be easily or directly convertible into the idiosyncrasies of another. This readily explains how Fascism acquired the criticism that it aims solely at the sharpening of national consciousness, nearly to the exclusion of all else and that its sole aims are center on the promotion of militaristic, expansionist interests.

Fascism is somewhat tragic because the more commonly accepted interpretations of the two most powerful Fascist regimes to rise before the onslaught of World War 2 are, in the main, accurate and correct. However, the proliferation of Fascism in other countries of that era only receives enough attention to draw connections between these various regimes and with Germany and Italy. Only the greatest intellectual and moral weakness would fail to recognize the atrocities committed by the Third Reich, or to associate those atrocities with genuine Fascism. However, the changes that occurred in Fascist methodology during World War 2 were largely ignored due to the constant need of the masses and their journalistic shepherds to find scapegoats. It is neither the purpose nor within the scope of this book to rehabilitate either Hitler or the National Socialists. It is my intent to present dominant themes and problems confronted by Fascism within and without and to lay out the fundamentals of an architecture for the future of my countrymen, my Nation, and my

Race.

21.

IMMIGRATION: A NATIONALIST APPROACH

Attitudes toward immigration policy have never lacked definition in this country. National policy toward immigration has zig-zagged from Left to Right and back again over the last 200 years. Many citizens have an attitude toward immigration, legal and otherwise, that is decidedly reactionary in the most basic sense of that word. Their reactions are decidedly hostile and understandable. Any country will cease to be a Land of Plenty when ceaseless and irresponsible immigration policy stretches jobs, space, and other resources to the absolute limit. We are approaching that limit. This is one of the issues brought to the forefront by the Democratic shell-game. Democracy puts no limits on freedom beyond prohibiting harm to others, all the while becoming more flexible and evasive in its definition of harm. It has opened the flood gates on immigration, allowing anyone with the gift of breathing to enter, accrue benefits they are not entitled to, and to stay here, displacing legitimate Americans and their culture.

Meanwhile on the left, mayors in large cities throughout the country and liberal-dominated legislatures are declaring "sanctuary" for illegal aliens. Please note my unlikely-to-change use of the outdated and politically incorrect term "illegal aliens". They are here illegally and they are alien to our country, our people, and our way of life. They do not belong here unless they can muster the discipline of mind to engage our due process in the way and manner in which it is meant to be utilized. However, as civilization's neglected children, these migrant populations have all the negative behaviors of children who have lacked proper parental supervision. Anything sneaky, underhanded, and antisocial becomes an imagine right the moment their feet touch American soil. While this is going on, liberals attack the government's stance on refugees, travelers from Muslim countries, and H-1B visas, and they bewail the legitimate enforcement of existing immigration laws. The left may have stopped short of endorsing open borders, but for decades they have treated opposition to illegal immigration and constraints on legal immigration as unacceptable, even racist.

Fascism opposes this anarchic concept of immigration with a social conception of race and immigration law. It does not permit that which harms the nation or its social harmony. Current sloppy thinking regarding legal and illegal immigration is harmful to the nation and its social harmony. Therefore, both must be stopped. Those who came here legally and acquired citizenship in the proper and legitimate manner must be given time to acculturate to the American milieu. Those who are here illegally must be given a matter of days to exit the country and apply properly for citizenship. Their living conditions while they are not citizens is not our concern. Furthermore, many of these people bring their conflicts with them. They certainly have done so in England and the United States. They also bring a cache of sneaky and underhanded behaviors. We give them unrestricted welfare benefits. They take this money and send it home.

In some cases, this money is used to fund terrorist activity. Wonderful! Americans are being compelled through their tax burden to purchase the knife that will be used to cut their throats. This is the legacy of liberalism. It permits everything and, in this age, actively promote the harm of private citizens living within the range of the Law. It is wrong. Give Nationalists half a chance and it will cease within a few months.

The default position of liberalism opposes resistance illegal immigration and maintains that legitimate constraints on immigration are morally wrong is harmful to the well-being of the Nation. Within the last 75 years, a powerful labor movement favored limits on immigration and fought against the justly-hated Bracero guest worker program, which imported Mexican laborers despite a healthy American labor pool from 1942 to 1964. Even labor organizers like Cesar Chavez supported the arrest and deportation of illegal farm workers. Chavez' union was composed primarily of Mexican-American workers. However, even Chavez' UFW recognized these operatives of Mexico's economic infiltration of the United

States as strike-breakers and scabs to be dealt with in the traditional, appropriate ways.

The anarchic freedom of liberal-infested democracy does not just permit the diversion of national resources such as tax revenues to the comfort of those who should not be here in the first place; it has still more harmful consequences. Regardless of who you may believe orchestrated the 9/11 attacks, the fact remains that the 9/11 terrorists slipped through an immigration net that is mostly holes and very little net. This is the lageacy of liberal-infest democracy. It exposes the Nation to inundations of desperate people who have neither the urge nor the inclination to act within our Laws. It exposes us all to higher violent crime rates, disease, terror, and very little that is of benefit to the Nation. The situation was little different during the waves of immigration that swept the country in the late 19th century. Foreigners were encouraged in the belief that our streets were paved with gold. When they arrived here, they learned the truth. An Italian saying summed up the disillusionment felt by many: "I came to America because I heard the streets were paved with gold. When I

got here, found out three things: First, the streets weren't paved with gold;

second, they weren't paved at all: and third, I was expected to pave them."

The truth of the matter, then as now, is that these waves of immigration

were an attempt by misguided politicians to import votes. Today, when

legitimate restrictions are placed on immigration numbers, unscrupulous

political operatives do much as the street gangs did during the 19th century

in fabricating votes. Whereas the cooping-gangs of the 19th century might

forcibly inebriate a man to get three or more votes out of him, today's

election criminals simply harvest the dead to get the election numbers they

need. In both cases, unscrupulous immigration practices supply an easy

alternative.

Illegal immigration wreaks havoc on our economy, our social harmony,

and on a culture already hard-pressed to rediscover its roots. It makes a

mockery of laws that are already marginalized. It is a disgrace to the

Nation and it criminalizes the one who engages in it. It makes legitimate citizens feel like they live in a country that everyone can invade and where laws are a joke. It is frontier anarchy; a brutal farce with the label "FREEDOM" stuck on it. To the undisciplined and uncivilized this freedom is like a drug you try once, get hooked on, and then you are abandoned in a wilderness state. Parasitic monsters batten onto this state. It is a stinking fens populated by swarms of harmful pests. We may import luminaries and professionals from other countries, but we import far more murderers, rapists, pedophiles, and future terrorists. We import them, "give" them rights, and then leave our legitimate citizens to deal with the new threat to their safety while lawmakers live in safe, gated communities replete with security staff.

The immigrant populations of the past may have chosen to live in segregated enclaves such as Little Italy, but they also chose to assimilate themselves to American society. English was spoken outside the home, even if it was learned with some difficulty. Wives were told by their husbands to learn to cook American dishes. The failure on our part lies not so much in our educating of immigrants in our schools (as education is largely aa failure for all groups), but in our hesitancy to inculcate values. The immigrant of today does not share in the greater vision of America because Americans have lost faith in that vision. The Promised Land no longer looms into view from the deck of a ship bringing immigrants to the New World. Today's immigrants seek to recreate here the country and the chaos they left behind. Why shouldn't they? America has been hollowed out; scrubbed clean of any cultural content that could be called truly and inherently American and replaced with the bland tabula rasa of political correctness, the fairy tale of white guilt, and generations of native-born deprived of their right to an identity. The immigrant coming to our shores will naturally be overwhelmed by our weakness and attempt to fill the void with their own perceived strengths. In this way, by sure and steady degrees, piece by piece, Americans are losing America.

MY STRUGGLE

When I was a child, my father effectively embraced me into a world of ideas, values, and history which he assured me that is my heritage and the heritage of all Americans. This world was grounded in the unchangeable and unchanging dominion of the Spirit. The particular German term for this is weltanschauung, denoting in part a particular philosophy or the world view of a particular group. I say in part because a weltanschauung is far more than a laundry list of particularized views. It is also the extra-temporal world one inherits that is formed of these views and moved, much as this physical globe is moved, by forces greater than mortal substance. This was the world of the West, formulated first in the cuneiform star tablets of ancient Sumer and Babylon. It possessed a spirit of inquiry and discovery imparted to it by the philosophers of ancient Greece, the architects of Egypt, the seafaring warriors of Northern Europe, and Legacies from the Celts, the Romans, the Iberians, Macedonians, Dacians, and many other races. It was a vast, rich tradition, bolstered by two thousand years of philosophy, architecture, laws, and even militarism. For only a fool would deny that struggle is central to man's heart.

My father died when I was very young and it seemed the world he taught me to believe in died with him. The very Earth beneath my feet seemed to become gelatinous and unstable. Ever a stubborn child, I refused to learn the lessons of circumstance because I knew they were beneath me and they angered me with their impertinence. I therefore vowed that I would give birth to that world in the circumstances of my young life. I wished to become God's Soldier; a Knight consecrated to a holy cause. I became very active in the Episcopal Church which I was too young to realize was infested with liberalism, cronyism, and many other things contrary to the teachings of Christ. I will not go into the long catalog the failures that church fed me instead of proper spiritual food. Suffice it to say that when my father died Christ's alleged minister was on vacation. That was 32 years ago, and it is simply wonderful to reflect on how a heavily liberalized institution created one of its own most dedicated foes. For I am completely opposed to all institutions that claim to represent that glorious

weltanschauung of which my father taught me and yet are doing all they

can to eradicate that world. The war is fought quietly, cunningly, each and

every day for decades, and if we do not climb out of the trenches we will be

gassed.

Much pain followed me through those years of my youth; some of it

spiritual, some of it physical. All of it was glorious because it ignited my

soul, which was all I had. In fact, the truth is my soul is all I have ever had.

Isn't that true of all of us? In any case, my father's death was the end of the

world and the beginning of my long initiation into pain and emptiness.

Today, there are two things of which my Reader can be assured: I am

absolutely sincere in what I am telling you and I know that you share that

pain and emptiness.

That initiation began in earnest when I entered basic training. I wanted to

be a soldier and a priest. I was searching for a path and I felt sure that my

path was going to lead me to become a chaplain in the United States Army.

I will spare you the uncomfortable details and simply tell you that, due to a

painful physical condition I was unable to pass basic training. This was

another failure to please my father; another incident in a life that I would

come to see as full of failures and not at all representative of that

transcendent world and weltanschauung I hoped to embody. My family

claimed to understand when I returned home an emaciated and confused

failure, but the truth is that civilization rejects its failures and I was one of

them. The ancient Spartans killed infants who were weak or mutant,

dashing them on the rocks. America pities its weaklings, putting them on

the community dole and marginalizing them. Who's the more cruel?

I had very few friends, and that is another story. What is pertinent here is

that I sought relief from my pain and entry into that world I was taught

was my heritage. At least, that is the story I told myself. In reality, I was only looking for an end to the pain, physical and spiritual. I wanted to no longer be a failure. I wanted to no longer be the stone the builders rejected. That was the nature of the fire that raged in me as my family pretended to understand. How could they understand? They swaddled themselves in the smugness of people who land on their feet. The same was true for virtually everyone I knew. They had comfortable lives (far more comfortable than many others!). Yet they looked with suspicion at all who had not attained their little versions of "paradise".

I took up with some young men I graduated high-school with. We drank, we worked, we smoked marijuana. I cannot and will not speak to the issues of my companions. I can only tell you that my first High seemed to take that world; that weltanschauung I had always believed in and made it mine. At least it made me believe so and the euphoria of marijuana was like a healing pain reliever to my soul. I had always had an active imagination and so the drug had a more psychotropic effect on me than my friends. It was almost hallucinogenic. I felt as if I had at last I been saved.

Anyone with an ounce of intelligence or common at this point in the narrative can discern easily the flaws in my reasoning during that time. Perhaps a few readers will sympathize. What was a major importance was the search, the hunger, and the burning desire for something greater than myself. I am no scholar of Asian languages, but I believe the Sanskrit word for what I was going through is tanha or thirst. However this is not the thirst of someone who is dehydrated. This is nothing less than the thirst for true and. authentic Being. That word is capitalized to set it apart from mere existence. To be is to live fully in touch with that world of which I have spoken; that weltanschauung whereby one is incorporated into a life of significance, principle, and tradition.

I had misidentified the Thirst that gripped me. I was in the grips of an active addiction to alcohol, tobacco, and marijuana. I neglected my responsibilities. I was bitter. I felt entitled. My father had died. Most of my relatives were concerned only with the temporary effect this had on them. The world of which I thought myself as an inheritor had failed to materialize. Life, as far as I was concerned, had failed me. Oh how I wanted to end the world; the world that had failed me. Me! They had no idea how special I was.

I was very blessed to hit bottom quicker than other people do. It only took me a couple of years before my family intervened and the gravity of my situation dawn on me. I got help. I cleaned myself up. It was not easy. In American culture, it is relatively easy to walk away from alcohol and marijuana. After all, America is a buffet of addictions. Sex, food, nicotine, caffeine, and thousands of ways to induce an adrenaline buzz or an unnatural release of endorphins are available in mass quantities. What is harder is to overcome the spiritual and existential side of addiction. I have been clean and sober for 25 years. I still have occasional days of struggle with "Tanha".

However, in time my sobriety began to take care of itself. This will no doubt make me a target for enthusiasts of a certain 12 step program, but that is not my concern. The way out of Darkness is light. The way out of ignorance is knowledge. The only choice for people who are lost and broken is to struggle, to strive for the next level at all times, add to temper oneself with discipline. That is the way to power.

At the age of 25 I found myself returning to college. I had tried to attend when I was 18, but I did not have the will to make it. After establishing myself in discipline, I returned. I did well. I did very well. My professors delighted in my enthusiasm and marveled at my consistent 4.0 average. It was a delightful struggle, and I even made friends along the way. However, my high grades and the friends I made were not what acted upon me in a formative way.

It was perhaps a measure of my own naiveté when, having been on campus for only a couple of days, I saw for the first time a young man with a piercing through the bottom of his lower lip. I thought he had been in some terrible industrial accident or shot with a low caliber pistol. However, I was soon to learn that this had become the fashion among young people. It must be understood that during the period of my dissolution, addiction and recovery from addiction I lived mainly in rural areas in a very sheltered way, out of touch with the fads of American pop culture. Just imagine my shock went on that same day, I saw a young man wearing a skirt. I do not mean a kilt. I mean a skirt. It was made of terry cloth, sported a paisley pattern and came down to his ankles. My revulsion at seeing these things was faint at that time. In retrospect, I must say that I unconsciously felt enraged by these things.

It was not long before I had my first encounter with homosexuals, hatred of white men, anti-Americanism and the unconventional sexual promiscuity that are part and parcel of the American college experience. Needless to say, the alcohol flowed like water. Hordes of young people were pissing away their parents' money at a bar with a 6-digit cover charge. Even among the professors a loose moral attitude was all the rage, to say nothing of the growing prominence of political correctness, revisionism of many kinds, and a distinct dislike for the world of tradition. I felt as if I had found Sodom and Gomorrah. My heart sank and most of the time I felt as if I had been punched in the stomach.

This grew when I had my first encounter with a forerunner of today's "social justice warriors". It was a young woman who made it clear from our first encounter that she found me repugnant, that she would not simply leave me alone, and that she would pick apart everything I said, usually beginning with a whiny retort of, "What's *that* supposed to mean?" I learned very quickly that the newly emerging social dispensation was about tolerance, but this tolerance was only for a handful of what would later be termed "protected classes" of which there can be none in a society that claims to be egalitarian. For one such as me, who believed in the weltanschauung of tradition, there was no tolerance; only extreme

prejudice at worst or, at best, a disdainful look, as if I were the hired help

that failed to disappear from the scene before the guests arrived for their

exclusive dinner party.

Not everything I experienced was so harsh. In the early days of my

academic experience, I enjoyed the heady Rush of postmodernist literature

and philosophy. In fact, I took on a dual major in English Literature and

Philosophy. I entertained dreams of one day getting my Ph.D and

becoming a tenured university professor. I felt sure that the best possible

contribution I could make to civilization was as a scholar, a writer, and a

poet. Before my 4 years of undergraduate study were over, I would see

how Destiny's plan is often at odds with our own.

As I approached graduation, I discovered that 4 years of having to defend

who and what I am had brought about a metamorphosis. On one level, I emerged as if from a cocoon where what I had assumed was the truth of my nature slept, or rather I had assumed it slept. On another level, when someone chisels away at a piece of stone, they are removing what is not the true nature of the stone to reveal what is. All those attacks on my heritage and my identity and this rough beast, slouching toward his birth emerged without fanfare and with a vengeance. I was a Fascist; ready and willing to defend who and what I am and my heritage as a son of the Western Tradition. I owed no one an apology. I owed no one an explanation. No one was getting one, either. I had walked through a long darkness.

My suffering was not at an end. I wound up homeless, though for a very brief time. I got myself an apartment. I worked, even earning myself a promotion to management. There was great joy in coming home to the dinky little hovel that my labors had paid for. It was mine. New dimensions of manhood unfolded as I savored lessons about frugality, prioritizing, and learning to cut through the bullshit I had cloaked myself in for years. It took a long time, but now I see the end product emerging, and that is probably not the end. What I held onto through all these stages was a burning desire for a true ideology. I desired truths of a spiritual nature that would nonetheless be pertinent to mental and physical life. I found them; not in some New Age bookstore, but in the teachings of the Fascists and Integralists. They offered me a lifeline out of my spiritual darkness and the morass of modern mediocrity.

Mediocrity is a dangerous narcotic. It produces a heavy sleep and many disorders in those who have been educated but not edified or initiated. It is the spiritual leprosy of our time, uploaded into the American mainframe as the status quo. Nobody believes anything strongly for fear of finding out they might be wrong. To be thought of as wrong today is to be excluded from discourse; to be marginalized completely; to be disprivileged to the point of being almost criminal. All belief is to be invested in the poorly understood bogey man that is democracy, and democracy gives no sense of purpose or transcendence. It is not a weltanschauung. It is sound without a voice; freedom without content; a face without features; life without merit.

We are encouraged to squander this life in cheap thrills, fads of the moment, and nothing deeper than a thimble. We are slaves to the ego, and that master is all too easily impressed with a few trinkets. We are narcissists who don't have sufficient vision to see that they hate what they see in the reflecting pool. When we drown it is not accidental.

What I discovered enabled me to live a life of significance. I have always known that I was of a certain, rare type. However, just because I live in a world where Matthew Arnold described my kind as, "wandering Between Two Worlds, one dead, the other powerless to be born," does not mean that I am condemned to a limbo where the world will never have to deal with me. I am real, I exist, and I will not be marginalized by the left, the GOP, or the rest of the sheeple. No matter how much faith and the religious impulse have being attacked, contradicted by science or political correctness, the Supreme Being guides my destiny and my destiny is still a valid reason to live. We are bound together, you and I, and we are all bound to National Destiny. Even if the world condemns us to the darkness, they cannot deprive us of the joys of self-discipline, self improvement, and the work of rebuilding what is still a great, young Nation. Our greatest days are still in front of us, the road ahead is long and we shall journey together, as will our descendants, from here to Empire.

In fascism I found a path for my life. It is a path open to all races. True fascism embraces Human Nature in its entirety and it refutes the idea that human nature is bound and determined by biology. Fascism Embraces the nation as a whole, involving the whole nation in its great work to mobilize the whole, to make every man and woman a pioneer in a new world and a new testament, and giving each the tremendous satisfaction of having fought and blend for a great, common ground. It showed me the greatness in my heart and pushed me to remove it from underneath the cover of Darkness. It showed me that. No matter what was done to denigrate the world and the weltanschauung that are my Birthright and yours, our true wealth can never be tarnished or devalued because it is priceless. This is not mere rhetorical gibberish. It is a way of life. Fascism endows the individual with the greatness of the task of civilization and thus it gives us

and inner Joy and vitality that cannot help but enlighten and transform the

entire world at large.

This is not a path of Conquest but of conquering. We seek to direct out

pioneering spirit toward our own country, ceiling out of borders and

bringing our troops back home. There is much work to be done here at

home. Our house is a mess and we presume to clean the world. The spirit

of fascism, directed into American society, will reveal to us a power and

glory we have never dreamed of. It will make advancement a prospect for

the talented who have proven their merit. It will rejuvenate our economy

by forcing us to make the greatest use of all our natural resources, the

greatest of which is the People. It will build Partnerships between workers

and management. It will restore a sense of sacred authority to the State

without basing that Authority on a state religion. It will put an end to racial

bitterness and ethnic squabbling by enforcing the peace, empowering each race two police and better itself and helping all to find their role in

National Destiny.

CPSIA information can be obtained
at www.ICGtesting.com
Printed in the USA
BVOW03s1955141117
500280BV00041B/509/P